"With this book, Joanne Lara and Susan Osborne present a comprehensive curriculum to prepare students with autism spectrum disorder to transition from school to employment. This interactive resource is an essential guide for teachers and caregivers working with young people to develop the necessary skills for getting and keeping a job."

—*Doreen Granpeesheh, CEO, Center for Autism & Related Disorders (C.A.R.D.)*

"Being part of Autism Works Now!® makes me feel more positive about the future and possibilities to help me reach my goals. That makes me happy."

—*Zachary Inkeles, author and artist, candidate, Autism Works Now!®, Los Angeles*

"Brilliant! This is essential reading for autism parents, educators and self-advocates. Joanne Lara and Susan Osborne have created the road map to successful employment in today's job market and—spoiler alert—preparation begins earlier than we were previously told! As an autism parent I am exceptionally grateful for this amazing tool. The work force needs these amazing, talented individuals, and they deserve the dignity and empowerment that comes with gainful employment!"

—*Shannon Penrod, host of Autism Live, producer of Autism in the Classroom*

"With an estimated 50,000 kids with autism reaching adulthood in the U.S. each year, thank you Joanne Lara and Susan Osborne for creating an innovative program to prepare these young adults for employment. With the help of Autism Works Now!® they will reach their full potential and lead independent, productive, meaningful lives. Hallelujah!"

—*Yudi Bennett, Co-Founder, Foothill Autism Alliance & Exceptional Minds*

"This is a much-needed resource that fills the gap in this country's school-to-job programs!"

—*Areva Martin Esq., President, Special Needs Network, USA*

"This book develops the skill set that our youth need in order to compete in the job force with dignity!"

—*Matt Asner, parent, advocate, VP at the Autism Society of America*

"Joanne Lara and Susan Osborne have created a comprehensive work readiness program with Autism Works Now!® and their Workplace Readiness Workshop. With this valuable resource, many individuals with autism will gain the ability to get and keep meaningful employment so they can go on to become valued members of their communities."

—*Alex Plank, autism advocate and Founder, WrongPlanet.net*

"Joanne Lara and Susan Osborne raise thought-provoking questions and unpack ideas relating to how we are preparing our students on the autism spectrum for life after high school. With this book, they lay the groundwork for educators and families who are helping young people develop the tools they need to work and live in the 21st century."

—*Dan Phillips, Transition Specialist,*
Culver City Unified School District

"This is the quintessential handbook for every teenager and young adult on the autism spectrum and their employers! It's a fabulous guide to making certain individuals with autism are successful in their careers and job search. Exactly what we need right now."

—*Susan Corwin, parent/advocate*

"Joanne Lara and Susan Osborne have created an innovative pre-employment program for young people with ASD that is like no other. My son, Christopher, had the good fortune to join Joanne and Susan's group Autism Works Now!® over a year ago and has gleaned extremely important and useful pre-employment skills and information that he was not privy to during his high school years. This book gives me hope that future generations of students leaving high school will be better prepared to meet the 'real world' of employment and social challenges that have previously been ignored by our educational system."

—*Pat Grayson-DeJong, M.Ed., parent and*
retired Autism Specialist, LAUSD

Teaching Pre-Employment Skills
to 14–17-Year-Olds

TEACHING PRE-EMPLOYMENT SKILLS TO 14–17-YEAR-OLDS

The Autism Works Now!® Method

Joanne Lara and Susan Osborne

Foreword by Temple Grandin

Jessica Kingsley *Publishers*
London and Philadelphia

Appendix 5 adapted from *The Complete Guide to Getting a Job for People with Autism Syndrome* (2013) by kind permission of Barbara Bissonnette.

Four Step SODA: Stop, Observe, Deliberate and Act on p.177 is reproduced by kind permission of Marjorie Bock.

First published in 2017
by Jessica Kingsley Publishers
73 Collier Street
London N1 9BE, UK
and
400 Market Street, Suite 400
Philadelphia, PA 19106, USA

www.jkp.com

Library of Congress Cataloging in Publication Data
A CIP catalog record for this book is available from the Library of Congress

British Library Cataloguing in Publication Data
A CIP catalogue record for this book is available from the British Library

ISBN 978 1 78592 725 6
eISBN 978 1 78450 378 9

Printed and bound in Great Britain

To my son Jacob, who has taught me more about love, patience, and hope than I ever thought possible, and my husband, Doug, who has always provided me with unconditional love and support. Susan Osborne

Contents

Part II: WORKSHOP STRUCTURE

Foreword

My sense of identity is based on my work. This is normal for lots of people. Many common surnames are also the names of occupations such as Cook, Mason, Carpenter, Smith, and Farmer. Being successful in my career has given my life purpose. I am what I do. When I was in my twenties, I wrote an article on how I made a slow transition from the world of school to the world of work. Too often students with autism spectrum disorders autism spectrum disorder (ASD) graduate from either high school or college and they have had no work experience. Work experiences should begin long before graduation. Students need to learn how to do tasks that are on a schedule. To be most effective, the tasks should be outside the immediate family. I want to emphasize it is never too late to start. If you are working with either a high school or college graduate who has not learned basic skills, he or she needs to be gradually eased away from the couch or the video games.

Mother knew how to stretch me, to try new things that were just outside my comfort zone. At age thirteen, she set up a sewing job with a freelance seamstress. Today, middle school-age children could walk dogs for the neighbors or do volunteer work at a church or community center. At age fifteen, after I had gone to a boarding school, they gave me the job of cleaning the horse stalls. I loved the responsibility of taking care of the horses. The following year I spent the summer at my aunt's ranch. Mother gave me a choice; I could go for a week or stay all summer. It is important to give the child some choices and I ended up loving the ranch and staying all summer. In college, I did two internships. One was at a research lab where I ran experiments. During this summer, I had to live in a rental house with

13

another person. The other was at a summer program for children with autism and I lived in a rented room. These internships were set up through local contacts. Throughout both college and graduate school I was doing freelance sign painting and learning more work skills.

During my career as a designer of livestock facilities, I have worked with many skilled trades people who were either dyslexic, had attention deficit hyperactivity disorder (ADHD) or were mildly autistic. They got and kept their jobs because they had both paper routes as young children and vocational training in high school. Parents need to work to get vocational skills back into the schools. Today there is a huge shortage of mechanics, welders, electricians, and plumbers. I worked with skilled trades people when they were building big Cargill and Tyson beef plants. These were big complex projects that required lots of brains to build them. My job was to design the cattle handling facilities. I have designed the front end of every Cargill beef plant in North America. A vocational career may be appropriate for about 25 percent of students with ASD or ADHD. Do not get hung up on labels. In fully verbal students, the diagnoses may switch back and forth between ASD and ADHD.

Parents and teachers must avoid the tendency to over protect and shelter students with ASD. I am seeing too many middle school and teenage students who have not learned basic skills such as shopping, because the parents always did it for them. This book has lots of advice on practical skills that students with ASD need to be taught. One basic skill that should be drilled in before graduation from high school is how to be on time. When I went to college, I had many social difficulties but being on time was not one of my problems. Once I had decided that I was going to study, I was on time. My science teacher gave me a reason to be motivated to study. Studying became important when I had the goal of becoming a scientist.

In conclusion, students must be willing to walk through the door of opportunity, when it opens. When I was asked to design the first dip vat (these are the projects that were shown in the HBO movie) I said yes because I wanted to prove that I was not stupid and that I could do it.

Sell yourself with a portfolio

I sold my design services by showing off a portfolio of drawings and photos of completed projects. The work must be neatly presented and you should always have it available on your phone or tablet. You never know where you might meet a person who can give you a job. Do not put too much stuff in your portfolio. You want a 30-second WOW when you show it to somebody. You need to target your audience. For example, do not show weird science fiction drawings when you are selling graphics to a client who has a car dealership. During interviews, I would open up my portfolio to sell freelance jobs. I learned to sell my work instead of myself. Having a career has given my life meaning. People a long time ago named their families after the names of occupations because it helped define who they were.

Preface

JOANNE LARA

Let's get out there and show people what people with autism can do!

Temple Grandin, Temple Grandin and Friends:
Autism Works Now! Event 2015 Los Angeles

Human resource interviewers should look beyond the resumes of individuals with autism and Asperger's when searching for qualified employees. With 50,000 individuals on the autism spectrum each year graduating from United States high schools with approximately an 80 percent unemployment rate, this population has proven to excel in 'splintered skill' sets, meaning they are often good at one job. For instance, they can excel in jobs such as computer graphics, computer science, coding, analytical calculations, patterns and inconsistencies, engineering and such, all highly regarded job qualifications that are specific to many employers' needs. The ASD population enthusiastically wants to work, be self-sufficient, and be contributing members of their communities.

If we begin to see job qualifications through different lenses, if we can reward individuals on the autism spectrum who have special talents in given areas, we can put to work these enthusiastic youths to work in often detailed types of jobs (in which they excel), and it's a win-win for everyone. Their problem is they often can't get through an interview because of their social difficulties, so human resource interviewers need to ferret out their interests and the kinds of things they not only like to do but can do beyond most expectations.

Prior to 1975, very few people were even thinking about how students with autism could be brought into the workforce because individuals with disabilities were not allowed to be educated in the public schools in most states in the United States before that time. The truth is that—after nineteen years of the institution of the Individual Transition Plan (ITP) being enacted as part of the Individuals with Disabilities Education Act (IDEA) 1997 (with 2004 subsequent transition revisions)—only a small percentage of our youth on the autism spectrum are transitioning into jobs in their communities, even though the primary goal of the ITP was and still is to assist our students into transitioning into the workforce after high school.

The IDEA 1997 and 2004 transition revisions were both well-meaning and direct descendants from the 1975 Public Law 94-142, but the program has to be viewed skeptically at best because less than 20 percent of all graduating students on the autism spectrum have jobs—even inconsequential jobs after high school—and the percentages become worse over time. Most go home and end up staying there, which is a human tragedy, anyway it's viewed. Sadly, this is known as the "School-to-Couch" model.

While unemployment for our youth with autism hovers at 80 percent, it is time that educators present a truthful idea of what the student is capable of doing for a living, which means that we might want to re-think the way that we are interpreting the ITP transitioning process, jobs, social opportunities in the community, and living accommodations after high school all together in this country. One of the reasons for these dismal statistics may be the lack of realism on the part of the Individualized Education Program (IEP) team members when they focus on the *Person Centered Planning* element, which concentrates on where the student's skill set in core reading and math actually lie and how this skill set can equate to a paying job.

IEP team members and, especially, parents often want to honor a student's dreams but—when that student's case history indicates that he/she will not be a scientist, an astronaut, a veterinarian, or have a three-picture deal at Warner Brothers Studio in Hollywood – we must ask ourselves if we are really indeed serving the student by entertaining these fantasy dreams of improbable employment. In reality, the student may be able to work in a vet's office or neighborhood shelter, gain employment on the Warner Brothers' lot, or work in a hospital, but the IEP team needs to be addressing practical job options for students who are not going to transition into a four-year college or a two-year community college. The students should be directed down a path that will give them a realistic idea of job options when they transition out of the public school setting.

The downfall of not entertaining realistic job options early on in the academic years is that, often, the student becomes attached to the fantasy job and the impractical idea of where he might actually fit in the job market. In the case of his/her vision of becoming a scientist, a vet, or an astronaut, the student can often be reluctant to want to pursue or seek jobs outside of these unlikely positions, even though other jobs could better meet his skill set and lifestyle, further contributing to the existing 80 percent unemployment statistic.

For the student who wants to be a scientist, why not have him/her research jobs that are available in a university science department? Or companies that do medical research? Or organizations where he can still be working in the area of her interest?

It is in the IEP team meetings that we need to begin to present a more realistic approach to job options for the student and begin to help him understand where he fits into the workforce. We stand a far better chance of getting the outside community employer's and stakeholder's support to help our youth be successful if we are realistic in how the student and the team view the student's potential, weighing in on his past success in the academic institution as a barometer for his future success. In addition, we all need to understand that there is a lack of vocational education in the middle and high school setting. Vocational education used to at one time be prevalent across the United States in all public schools; woodworking, metal working, car repair, bakery skills, care detailing, horticulture, animal husbandry—these courses could be found in any high school. The Smith-Hughes Act of 1917 was the law that first authorized federal funding for vocational education in American schools and explicitly described vocational education as "preparation for careers not requiring a bachelor's degree." Vocational education was not designed to prepare students for college rather it was to prepare the student to work in a job force that required a certain specific skill set.

What happened to vocational training? In the late 1990s and early 2000s, the standards and accountability movement in the school systems was taking hold, so the states had begun to write academic standards or goals for what students should learn and, in the process, what wasn't critical to the learning and, in many cases, what was needed or not needed to obtain funding of the educational process.

Then in 2001, Congress passed the "No Child Left Behind" Act. That law required states to test their students every year and to ensure that all students would eventually be proficient in math and reading in exchange for federal education funding. This was the beginning of the end of vocational training in this country (American RadioWorks 2014).

The majority of vocational schools didn't meet the academic faculty "highly qualified educator" requirements in order to meet the No Child Left Behind criterion. While vocational educators had the skilled labor experts to teach the skills like metalworking, woodworking, horticulture, bakery, culinary arts, car detailing, cosmetology, and so on, the instructors themselves did not have the diploma in the discipline to fulfill the No Child Left Behind Act's standards. So, the very skill sets that could most benefit our youth on the autism spectrum, because what they would learn in vocational training could be turned into meaningful jobs, are basically no longer available in the public school setting in the United States.

In other words, for those students in the academic school setting and who have an IEP (a document that is developed for each public school child in special education) a member of the IEP team can assess and tell us what the student is good at or could be good at doing that would allow him to get a job once he graduates from high school. However they cannot teach him that skill set because the majority of the schools do not have the vocational centers any longer that provide the facilitation to educate the student in the skill set that the assessment indicates would serve him best.

In addition, the vocational programs (e.g. computer science; animation; art; home economics; shop; drafting; advertising/layout/ design; photography; economics, banking, budgeting, etc.) that go hand in hand with teaching independent living skills currently only exist in the Moderate/Severe Special Day Programs. These programs are typically not available for our Asperger's and higher functioning students with autism, who can also benefit from vocational training if they are to live self-determined lives after high school.

What can be done?

- The ITP must be started early in the schools—at 14 years of age—but parents need to have a vision for their child's future beginning in kindergarten and the early elementary school years. Everyone who is a member of the child's team, including the student himself, needs to be creating an idea of who this person is, what his capabilities are in his home, his community and what is his place in the world now and in the future. We do it for our neurotypical children. Why are we not doing it for our children with autism? Because we feel guilty? Because we ourselves are not certain that indeed there is a place for him in the community? In the job force? If this is the case, then we must work harder, yell louder, make our voices heard, that we want our youth with autism to have realistic choices for employment, options for social activities and outings in the community and alternatives to the 'School–to-Couch' living model.

- If there is an opportunity to bring back vocational programs into the public schools—even if your child isn't oriented toward vocational education—support the effort, because it will benefit jobs for thousands of individuals, whether or not they're on the autism spectrum.

- At as early a time as possible while the child is still in high school, parents will need to evaluate and consider vocational schools for their post-high school graduate, linking his interest and job skill sets to what is offered in vocational schools.

- Many of the subjects that provide great jobs and incomes are taught in junior colleges, such as agriculture/plant management; cosmetology; nursing assistant/home health care; computer science; automobile mechanics; restaurant/food services. If they don't exist in your community, consider other close-by communities, because many junior colleges house specialty programs, depending upon their locations (e.g. some of the best schools in cuisine/restaurant/food services are in major metropolitan area junior colleges).

- Look at specialty schools like the Art Institute and Design Schools; retail training and management programs; accounting, electrical, plumbing, and a host of other high-end salary possibilities.

- Check out programs that transition students after high school into the workforce or into college, if that's the goal, where learning to keep a budget, take care of themselves, and live independently are cornerstones of the program.

Why aren't our students on the autism spectrum ultimately transitioning into jobs when the ITP should work?

In June 2014, only 19.3 percent of people with disabilities in the US were participating in the labor force—working or seeking work. Of those, 12.9 percent were unemployed, meaning only 16.8 percent of the population with disabilities was employed. By contrast, 69.3 percent of people without disabilities were in the labor force, and 65 percent of the population without disabilities were employed (United States Department of Labour, Bureau of Labor Statistics 2017). We may need to ask ourselves: what is wrong with the current education picture? We spend an enormous amount of time assessing, teaching reading and math proficiencies, and making sure that the student is prepared for life after high school only to find that the statistics are against him. To summarize, the options after high school for our youth fall into four categories.

1. attend a special day program in the community where they generally develop life skills, go out into the community as a crowd, and often work either independently or as a group in a supported job environment

2. enroll in a community two-year or four-year college program with support provided by the regional center and the university or college Disability Support Services Center

3. transition into a part-time or full time job, or

4. shift to a residential program where they learn the additional job readiness skill sets that they can take into the community that will hopefully equate to employment.

Universities in order to be federally compliant must have a Disabilities Support Services Center that the student registers with when they enroll in the college. The Disabilities Support Services Center assesses the student and together the college and the student decide what accommodations are needed in order for the student to be successful in the college setting: for example, does the student require a sign language interpreter, a note taker, extended time for assignments, extended due dates for tests, extra time to get to classes? Proximity to the instructor is considered, all the very same modifications that were available to the student when he was in the public school setting. Typically, by this time in the student's life he has reached the age of majority, when a young person is considered to be an adult. Depending on state laws this can happen between 18 and 21 years of age. At this juncture in a child's life, the state may transfer to that child all (or some of) the educational rights that the parents have had up to the moment. Not all states transfer rights at age of majority.

However, a state must establish procedures for appointing the parent of a child with a disability, or, if the parent is not available, another appropriate individual, to represent the educational interests of the child throughout the period of the child's eligibility. If under state law a child who has reached the age of majority and has not been determined to be incompetent, can be determined not to have the ability to provide informed consent with respect to the child's educational program, then that representative will make the decisions.

Some programs are specifically transitional, meaning they are teaching life skills like budgeting, transportation, living with others outside the home, and college-level preparation coursework. Attending college requires students to develop self-determination skills, self-management, self-advocacy and social skills, along with self-monitoring in order to excel and be successful. Some basic planning strategies for college should include the following:

•   Parents should register their child with the college of their choice and provide all the required documentation for registration. In order to receive special accommodation as mandated by the Americans with Disabilities Act (ADA), it is important to register with the College Disability Services.

- Families should be familiar with ADA, which mandates the laws as to how colleges must accommodate people with disabilities.

- Additionally, parents need to know if there is a special room in the dormitory or assigned location where their child can go during sensory meltdowns.

- Staff responsible for the dormitory should be trained and educated on the needs of students with special needs. They must be aware of the accommodations necessary to make the college experience a pleasant one.

Paul Hippolitus, Director of Disabled Students Program, University of California Berkeley developed a course called C2C+ or "Bridging the gap from college to careers" that is a university/community 17-lesson model that includes internships, peer and career mentoring, and placement assistance for individuals with disabilities. The course is offered at UC Berkeley, Silicon Valley Business Leadership Network, Orange County Business Leadership Network, San Diego State University and San Diego Business Leadership Network. More and more of these types of programs are becoming available to our students with autism across the country, filling the void that is left when they exit the public school setting at 18 or 22 years of age and transition into a secondary education or community setting and find that they are not prepared to compete in either arena.

Introduction

What is an Individualized Transition Plan (ITP)? Should the student be attending?

The ITP process requires that the student must be invited to the ITP meeting, because the plan should be put together to prepare the child for life. The process takes place generally at the age of 16, but some states, like California, North Carolina and Texas, begin earlier at age 14. The secondary transition planning is a federal mandate, first authorized in IDEA 1997, and it was reauthorized in IDEA 2004 specifying that the transition services are to begin by 16 years of age instead of the 1997 mandate which was 14. It also included a "coordinated set of activities designed within a result-oriented process" focused on improving both academic and functional achievement of the student with a disability to facilitate movement from school into post school life (Individuals with Disabilities Education Act IDEA 1997).

The student should be a part of the process because the transition services should be based on the individual's needs, which should also take into account the student's preferences and interests.

The ITP must include appropriate, measurable, post-school goals based upon age-appropriate transition assessments. Transition services include:

1. Instruction ~ Academic or vocational instruction that will assist the student in obtaining a career path;

2. Related services ~ Occupational Therapy; Behavioral; Speech and Language, along with Adaptive Skills;

3. Community experiences ~ Outings in the community (Community-Based Instruction, CBI);

4. The development of employment and other post school adult living objectives;

5. Acquisition of daily living skills (when appropriate);

6. Functional vocational evaluation (when appropriate).

The ITP includes more accountability on the part of the school, and it also makes it clear that the ITP is not intended to be an activity that just occurs once a year at a student's IEP meeting. Transition planning should be ongoing throughout the student's academic years, thus making key players out of the roles of the parent, the educators, the service providers, and the administration in assisting the student in making a smooth transition from school to the job force and his community.

The ITP helps students develop independence. The student should not only be attending their IEP/ITP meetings; he should be playing an active role in the meeting. When the IEP/ITP process and the team are looked at as being proactive, this in turn helps the student reach his career and adult-living goals faster. Transition planning should occur near the end of middle school, when the student begins planning his or her high school course of study.

The goal should be for all our individuals to be independent and self-determined to obtain and keep a meaningful job. We want to move away from everyone doing everything for our individuals with disabilities to advocacy that is self-motivated and self-driven. As the saying goes, "Give a man a fish and you feed him for a day. Teach a man to fish, and you feed him for a lifetime."

Part I

UNDERSTANDING AUTISM WORKS NOW® METHOD

Chapter 1

The Importance of Work

When I get a full time job in my field of interest, I will feel like I've really accomplished something.

Luke Guastaferro

When you meet someone at a party, usually one of the first questions asked is "What do you do?" For most of us, what we do is what we do for work. If we like our job, it's the essence of who we are. We'll say we are architects, accountants, and auto mechanics. We are the successful CEO of a multinational corporation or the principal of the local high school.

If we don't like our job, we usually dream of doing something we like. Especially in Los Angeles, many waiters and waitresses aspire to work in the entertainment industry. When asked the question "What do you do?" they'll say they are an actor, writer, or filmmaker. Their identity is not as an employee of the restaurant where they work. They see themselves as a successful professional in an industry where they want to be recognized and compensated for their talents and abilities.

Of course, making money is the primary reason why most of us get a job. It gives us the financial means to provide for ourselves and our families. Our well-being is greatly improved when we can afford to pay for all our basic needs like food, lodging, shelter, and transportation and still have money left over to enjoy the things we like. We can save up for a much-needed vacation, finance the car of our dreams, and enjoy a night out at the movies watching the latest blockbuster or indie thriller.

Another reason why we work is to provide a structure to our day. It's the reason why we get out of bed in the morning and go to sleep at night at a reasonable hour. If we work in an office, we arrive at nine, go to lunch at noon, and leave at five. We look forward to our time off. Wednesday is hump day and TGIF means that Friday and the weekend are almost here. We use our paid time off when work is slow, and we make plans on holiday weekends to get out of town and spend time with family and friends.

But does more money make us happier? Researchers Daniel Kahneman and Angus Deaton analyzed over 450,000 responses from a daily survey of 1000 United States residents looking at their feelings of emotional well-being and levels of happiness. They concluded that respondents with incomes under $75,000 reported lower levels of well-being and more of life's misfortunes like divorce, ill health, and feelings of loneliness. Respondents with incomes over $75,000 reported higher levels of well-being but did not report greater levels of happiness. So, this means that once we have enough income to cover our basic living expenses, our jobs need to have meaning for us to be happy (Kahneman and Deaton 2010).

What is meaningful work?

While it is important to have a job that pays us enough money to cover our bills plus a little extra, it is equally important that we feel a connection to our work. Ideally, we land a job in our field of interest with people we like for a company that values what we do. Every person has interests and values that are specific to both their field of work and the people with whom they work, so the definition of meaningful work is specific to that individual.

The area of study around the concept of meaningful work is now being examined by psychologists. Michael Steger, Associate Professor in Counseling Psychology and Applied Social Psychology at Colorado State University, has done research on this topic, and he concludes that meaningful work has three central components.

1. Our work must make sense. We must understand what's being asked of us and be provided with the appropriate resources to do our job.

2. Our work must fit within a larger context. We must understand the purpose of our work and how our daily tasks are connected to the mission of our company.

3. Our work must benefit some greater good. We must feel that our work is making a difference in the lives of others. This can be as grand as working to save the planet or as basic as volunteering to help shelter animals.

In other words, for our work to have meaning, we must:

1. understand what we must do and how to do it

2. know how the work we do fits into the larger picture

3. see that our work creates a benefit for someone outside ourselves. (Steger 2009, p.212)

Dr. Steven Wright takes this concept even further. He proposes that if people learn about the processes within their company or institution, they're more likely to do their jobs well, understand how their work fits with what other workers are doing, and how the product of their efforts creates value. This leads to a sense of meaning, which in turn makes people better at what they do (Wright 2009). Patrick McKnight and Todd Kashdan apply meaningful work in a larger context, pointing out that "Living in accord with one's purpose offers a person the opportunity to find a self-sustaining source of meaning through goal pursuit and goal attainment. Meaning drives the development of purpose, and once a purpose becomes developed, purpose drives meaning" (McKnight and Kashdan 2009). In other words, once people find meaning in their work, they find their life's purpose.

Why are friends important in a job search?

We are nowhere without friends. The essence of who we are as a civilization is based on the quality of our friendships. Without people in our lives that we can depend upon, we become isolated from our communities, which leads to destructive feelings of isolation, loneliness, and depression.

School is the first place where most of us find friends. It provides us with a structured environment and a place to meet and see our friends every day. From preschool through high school, we develop meaningful friendships through shared interests. In college, we find friends in classes based on our shared major and through campus activities. After we graduate, some of these friendships go on to last a lifetime. These friends become our colleagues who often refer us to available jobs within our shared field.

After college, as adults, we spend most of our time at work, as the United States Bureau of Labor Statistics Time Use Graph indicates (United States Department of Labor, Bureau of Labor Statistics 2016b; see Figure 1.1). The graph tells us that work takes up the largest part of the day at 8.8 hours, followed by sleeping at 7.8 hours, then household activities, followed by leisure and sports at 2.6 hours.

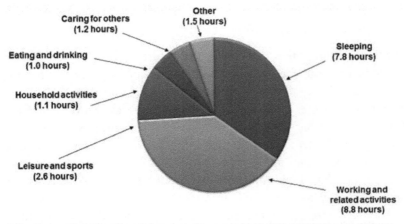

NOTE: Data include employed persons on days they worked, ages 25 to 54, who lived in households with children under 18. Data include non-holiday weekdays and are annual averages for 2015. Data include related travel for each activity.
SOURCE: Bureau of Labor Statistics, American Time Use Survey

Figure 1.1 Time use on an average work day for employed persons ages 25 to 54 with children

Since as adults we spend most of our day at work, it makes sense that this is where we find most of our friends after high school and college. Friends at work make the day more enjoyable, and they help us out when we need it. They are the people that we like to hang out with at lunch and after work and make plans with on the weekends. Not having a job limits our opportunities to meet the kind of people that we can learn to depend upon and care about.

Research shows that most jobs are secured through referrals. A report by the Federal Reserve Bank of New York concluded that between 52 percent and 58 percent of male workers under the age of 45 learned about their current job from a friend or relative. For first-time jobs, the percentage increased from 55 percent and 67 percent.

The report also stated that referred candidates were hired at a higher percentage, experienced an initial wage advantage, stayed on the job longer, and were more productive than non-referred workers (Brown, Setren, and Topa 2012).

How are individuals with autism affected in their ability in finding and keeping a job?

Autism Speaks, a United States advocacy organization dedicated to autism research, awareness, and outreach, describes ASD as "a group of complex disorders of brain development characterized in varying degrees by difficulties with social interactions, verbal and nonverbal communication, and repetitive behaviors" (Autism Speaks 2016). There are no medical tests that can determine if an individual has autism. Instead, a trained professional (usually a therapist or psychologist) uses autism-specific assessments and evaluations to make the determination. Autism can be accompanied by comorbid medical or psychiatric conditions, which can make it difficult develop an accurate diagnosis and an effective treatment plan. How much an individual is affected by their autism is specific to the individual and can vary greatly.

By far the biggest challenge for individuals with autism is the area of social communication. Communication development for children with autism happens, but differently and more slowly than it does for their non-autistic peers. Throughout their lifespan, individuals can have difficulties reading verbal and nonverbal social cues as well as making eye contact. Individuals with high functioning autism may be able to comprehend the thoughts and feelings of others but their social responses are often not typical or expected.

Another big challenge for individuals with autism is their difficulty in understanding the emotional states and corresponding thoughts, intentions, and feelings of other people. This is called "Theory of Mind," a concept that was developed by researcher Simon Baron-Cohen, Professor of Developmental Psychopathology at the University of Cambridge in the United Kingdom, Director of the University's Autism Research Centre, and a Fellow of Trinity College. Baron-Cohen concluded that children with autism suffer from "mindblindness" or the inability to be able to interpret what others are feeling or thinking because of a selective impairment in mindreading, and, for these children, the world is essentially devoid of mental things (Baron-Cohen 1997).

Many individuals with autism have problems with their capacity to stay organized, complete tasks, and adapt to new ways of doing things. They tend to be good at retaining facts and pieces of information, but they have challenges applying information to a larger context. This results in a difficulty in "seeing the big picture" also known as "gestalt." These types of skills fall under the term "executive functioning," but "executive functionings" is a more accurate description because the term covers a variety of different functions. As cited by Paula Moraine, executive functionings are a "set of mental processes that help connect experience with present action. People use it to perform activities such as planning, organizing, strategizing, paying attention to and remembering details, and managing time and space" (Moraine 2015, p.93).

Many individuals with autism have a dysregulation in their sensory system, which can make them over- or under-responsive to elements in their environment. They may be impacted in their vestibular system, which affects their ability to balance, or their proprioceptive system, which affects their ability to sense where their body is in space. Because of the way that the brains of these individuals process sensory information, they may find ordinary situations overwhelming, which can cause them to withdraw from daily activities.

All the unique challenges faced by individuals with autism have a direct impact on their ability to secure and sustain meaningful employment. If a person has a hard time forming friendships, job referrals don't materialize. If they are successful in getting a job, they may behave in ways that aren't expected by their coworkers, which can interfere with their ability to form friendships and workplace alliances. If they have difficulty understanding the thoughts and feelings of their coworkers and supervisors, they will have a hard time anticipating what they are expected to do. Problems with time management make it tough to get to work promptly and know when to return from break. Having challenges understanding the big picture makes it difficult to understand the importance of our job. As research, has shown, understanding how and what we bring to our work and how it fits within our company's big picture is often a prerequisite for us to find meaning in our work. Without this, individuals with autism can have difficulty finding their life's purpose.

How is autism treated and how can the basis of those treatments assist individuals with autism in the workplace?

Because individuals with autism are affected in ways that are specific to each one, it is said that if you meet one individual with autism you have met one individual with autism. Support plans must include interventions that are tailored to address each of the specific core deficits or needs. Step by step instruction, or a task analysis (breakdown of a skill set with instructions for each step of the process) when learning a new skill can be beneficial. When we break down larger tasks into smaller components we can often learn the skill faster.

A universal challenge for individuals with autism is their ability to generalize the use of acquired skills across multiple environments, meaning to replicate a skill learned in one environment in a totally new setting. For instance, mastering how to operate a scanning machine in one office building then being asked to perform the task of scanning papers in a totally different office building for a new company or organization can become problematic, with the individual not knowing which step to perform first. In this case, the skill set of scanning documents need to be re-taught in the new setting.

Teaching a skill in the classroom is the beginning but it is usually not enough for the individual to be proficient when the skill set is required in a new setting. It needs to be practiced multiple times in a variety of community-based settings so the individual can retain what they've learned and improve upon the skill over time. Teaching workplace readiness skills in a classroom setting is a good way to introduce concepts like proper workplace attire, appropriate conversation topics, and the essentials of interview preparation. With appropriate supports, a facilitated meeting with a business professional or human resource director is an excellent opportunity for the individual to practice the skills that they've been taught in an actual workplace setting.

The reason why treatments for autism are effective lies in the unique structure of the brain itself. In *Autism Movement Therapy Method®: Waking Up the Brain!* Joanne Lara tells us that:

> Our brain has the amazing natural capacity to compensate for injury or disease throughout our life. The ability to reorganize and form new connections, synapses (chemical or electrical connection points between brain cells), or create neural pathways in our nervous system

is called "neuroplasticity." Though controversial, the science of neuroplasticity is based on the idea that the adult brain can improve cognition and/or restoring lost mental abilities and function through regular, continual physical and mental activities. (Lara 2015)

After the individual is placed in a job, a job coach who is knowledgeable about autism is essential for the person to be successful. The role of a job coach is like that of a behavioral interventionist. The behavioral interventionist supports children with autism at school, at home, and in the community to help them achieve their behavioral goals. A job coach supports individuals with autism in the workplace so they can achieve their goal of maintaining meaningful employment. Once the individual can do their job with minimal support and has developed a positive working relationship with at least one of their coworkers, supports are reduced and, when possible, eliminated altogether. Regular job evaluations are an effective way to help the individual receive constructive criticism about their job performance and reflect on ways to improve.

What are hard and soft job skills and how do these skills affect individuals with autism in the workplace?

Skills that are specific to a job are called hard skills and are typically acquired in college, vocational training programs, and trade schools. But workers must have skills beyond the technical knowledge required by the job. They must be good at interpersonal communication, decision making, and problem-solving. These are called soft skills and are transferrable to any workplace. To keep a job, an employee must have the hard skills needed to get the job done along with the essential soft skills to keep the workplace running smoothly, efficiently, and conflict free.

For individuals with autism, acquiring hard skills for a job may be a relative strength due to the unique wiring of the structure of their brain which makes it easy for them to retain facts and compile information. Conversely, learning soft skills is a universal challenge for almost everyone on the autism spectrum. This means that an effective job training for this population requires not just teaching the technical skills for the job but also facilitated instruction of the essential soft skills to help them get along and connect with coworkers, plan and organize job responsibilities, and learn how to self-advocate in the workplace.

What more can be done to help individuals with autism succeed in the workplace?

Autism Works Now (AWN) believes that understanding leads to acceptance, and once employers and people in the workplace are aware of what autism is and the contributions that these individuals can bring to the workplace, they will be more accepting and open to working with individuals with autism. To achieve this goal, autism awareness education needs to be provided to supervisors and coworkers who will be working directly with the individual. Through these efforts, AWN believes that the result will be workplace environments that are accepting and welcoming of the differences of all their employees, not just their employees with autism.

Why is it important to teach workplace readiness skills to middle and high school students with autism?

As discussed earlier, to adequately support our youth with autism for a successful transition into their adult lives, ITP goals must be established starting in middle school so that the student can be supported in creating an effective transition plan when they transition out of the high school setting. While some students might be able to obtain a university degree, other students may be better suited to attending a trade school or community college where they can learn a vocational trade. Internships and volunteer jobs with proper supports provide excellent opportunities to help these students gain essential job skills, develop professional contacts, and find meaning in the work they are doing.

How can we address the unmet needs of middle and high school students with autism and their ability to secure and sustain meaningful employment?

To help students accomplish their ITP goals, it is essential to start teaching vocational and pre-employment skills starting in middle school. The most effective method of training incorporates classroom instruction with authentic community-based learning opportunities so they can put into practice the skills they've learned. For these students to be engaged in the learning process, we must create a fun and safe environment where they are provided an opportunity to discover the importance of what they are learning. They must be active participants in the learning process so what they are learning takes on meaning for them.

How does the AWN Method accomplish these goals?

The Workplace Readiness Workshop was developed by AWN to provide an interactive learning environment to help individuals with autism acquire the pre-employment skills needed to secure and sustain meaningful employment. The workshop runs over eight months with each month consisting of three classroom meetings and one community-based field trip.

Why are participants in the AWN program called candidates?

AWN believes that words are powerful, and we want our participants to view themselves as a viable member of the work community. To help them envision themselves in this light, we address participants as candidates. AWN recommends that a program tailored for middle and high school students can also use the term "candidates" to address the students in their program.

What is the format of classroom meetings?

There are four parts to each classroom meeting and each part has a purpose.

Part 1: Agenda and Introductions

The agenda is reviewed and any guests that are visiting the class are introduced now. The introduction lasts about five minutes.

Part 2: Roundtable Discussion

In a group discussion, candidates practice sharing information about themselves, remembering information about other candidates, assess their internal state of mind, and practice stress management.

THE IMPORTANCE OF WORK

Candidates are paired with a peer to practice their conversational skills and learn about conversational topics that are appropriate in the workplace. Occasional guest speakers are scheduled during this time in the session. The Roundtable Discussion lasts between 35 and 40 minutes.

Part 3: Prepare and Practice

Each month, information on a new workplace topic is presented and discussed. Candidates are supported in planning and preparing for upcoming field trips and group activities. Prepare and Practice lasts between 35 and 40 minutes.

Part 4: Recall and Review

To help candidates recall what was covered during the workshop, the group reviews what was addressed in class that day. Candidates also take a quiz at the end of the session about information that was covered in the workshop for that session. The short quiz contains a mixture of five true or false and multiple choice questions. Recall and Review lasts between 10 and 15 minutes.

What is the format of field trips?

All field trips take place in the workplace of a local company. Candidates are prepped in advance of the field trip in class to review what they should wear, decide upon their method of transportation to the field trip, and conduct internet research on the establishment or organization that they will be visiting. Each candidate is assigned a question to ask during the field trip meeting and as a group after the field trip, a group thank you email is sent to the field trip host or director.

How is this book formatted?

The AWN method book is divided into two parts:

Part 1 reviews the topics featured in Roundtable Depression and Prepare and Practice and how candidates can be helped to generalize the use of the soft and hard skills sets that are taught in the workshop.

Part 2 provides information about the nuts and bolts of the AWN Workplace Readiness Workshop and how to adapt a similar program in any community. Information is included on how to create a safe learning environment, behavioral management techniques, room and equipment requirements, and the structure of class meetings and field trips. Teacher instructional materials include classroom meeting agendas and presentation templates. The final chapter contains a copy of all instructional documents that are referenced throughout the book along with how to organize a candidate AWN workshop binder.

How does the book accommodate for the needs of middle and high school students with autism?

The authors, Joanne Lara and Susan Osborne, have years of experience working with individuals with autism of all ages, from toddlers to adults. The workshop was created to meet the needs of adults with autism to help them acquire the skills they need to secure and sustain meaningful employment. Most of the materials used in the workshop are also appropriate for middle and high school aged students, but, when needed, they have been modified considering the student's status as a minor and how the role of a parent of a minor child with autism is different from that for a parent of an adult child with autism.

Chapter 2

Matching the Job to the Individual and Filling in the Blanks

How to Assess an Individual's Interests, Skills and Abilities
for Job Placement and Workplace Paperwork

The best way to be productive in your job is to love what you do.

Luke Rose

Even the most accomplished people in the business world started work in an entry-level job. Warren Buffett, CEO of Berkshire Hathaway who has a net worth of $58.5 billion, was a paperboy. Oprah Winfrey worked at a corner grocery store next to her dad's barber shop. President Barack Obama scooped ice cream at a Baskin-Robbins.

Just like these highly successful individuals, most of us didn't view our first job as one where we would stay employed for our entire working lives. Our first job was a place where we could make some money, gain some work experience, and meet new people. Our job helped us to learn many important life skills like budgeting, time management, working with others, and understanding the value of hard work. Our first job was also an important part of our transition to adulthood because it provided us with an opportunity to become a member of a community separate and apart from the family we knew growing up.

Why is it important to match an individual with autism to a job that is suited to their interests, skills, and abilities?

To find purpose in our lives, we need to have a meaningful connection to the work that we do. To do this, we need to like our work and find it interesting. Our level of job satisfaction is a direct result of these two factors, and once we find satisfaction in our work, we often find our life's purpose.

Individuals on the autism spectrum have the same need to feel a meaningful connection to their job and like what they do. In fact, it may be even more important to place them in jobs that are connected to their special interests. Many of these individuals are highly knowledgeable about one specific subject. This is referred to as having splintered skill sets, and this type of extreme knowledge in one specific area or reservoir of information can be an asset for companies and organizations that specialize in work related to that topic. This hyper-focus can also present challenges in job placements. Because their level of interest can be very intensified, it may be difficult for the individual to be motivated to do something they don't like or that falls outside their area of interest.

How do you determine an individual's interests, skills, and abilities?

Assessments are the best way to identify what the individual likes to do and the types of jobs that would be a good match for their abilities, skills, and interests. In the Workplace Readiness Workshop, we use five assessments to get an understanding of who the candidate is and the type of work that would be meaningful to them.

An overview of the assessments used by AWN is included below and a copy of each assessment is included in the final chapter. There are many more assessment tools available so feel free to incorporate any that you think will work best in meeting the needs of the individuals that you are supporting or have enrolled in your program. The goal is to complete these within the first one to two months to establish each candidate's baseline work knowledge, skill set levels, and types of jobs that each would be best suited. These assessments also provide a way to evaluate the types and amount of support a candidate will need to successfully participate in the workshop.

Beginning in middle school, students need to be assessed to determine the types of jobs that would be a good match for their interests, skills, and abilities. It's also essential that every student be supported through the end of high school in selecting the best classes that will help them accomplish their career and vocational goals.

When looking to secure a location for a field trip, try to match companies to places where candidates would eventually like to work. These meetings provide them with insight into a business where they would like to work and help them to develop a professional contact in their field of interest.

General Work Knowledge

This was developed by AWN to assess each candidate's baseline general work knowledge, technical abilities, and general knowledge about the interview process.

How to interpret the results

This assessment provides a snapshot of the candidate's competence in using a computer, past work or volunteer experience, their skill in using email, and competency in using workplace software. It will also help in determining the amount and type of supports a candidate may require during class and on field trips.

When to administer

Candidates should complete this assessment during the first meeting of the workshop and again during the last month. Comparing the results of both assessments will determine how much knowledge a candidate has acquired throughout the workshop.

Google Knowledge

This is used to determine a candidate's proficiency in the use of Google and its many free apps with include Gmail, Drive, Contacts, Calendar, Maps, and Tasks.

How to interpret the results

These are used to help determine each candidate's competency level using Google and the apps that we use in class. For candidates who are not competent using a computer or office software, the results are used to identify the type and level of support each candidate will require during class so they can fully participate in the workshop.

When to administer

Candidates should complete this assessment during the first and last month of the workshop. Comparing the results of both assessments will determine how much knowledge about Google and its apps that the candidate has retained.

Preferred Workplace Profile

The **Preferred Workplace Profile** [5] is used by AWN to identify a candidate's preferred workplace environment and desired workplace characteristics.

How to interpret the results

This assessment will identify the types of workplace environments that are best suited to each candidate. The results will be useful in determining the focus of a candidate's job search and determining the types of placements would be a good fit for the candidate.

When to administer

Candidates should complete the Preferred Workplace Profile during the first month of the workshop.

Interests Inventory

This **Interests Inventory** assessment [4] was developed by AWN to identify a candidate's top interests, leisure activities, and things they like to do for extended periods of time. It is used to identify common interests among candidates in the group.

How to interpret the results

This assessment will identify the interests of each candidate and help candidates identify which interests they share with other members of the group.

When to administer

The Interests Assessment should be completed by candidates during the first month of enrollment. The results are used throughout the workshop to help candidates recall information about other members of the group.

Work Smarts—Using Multiple Intelligences to Make Better Career Choices

The **Work Smarts Assessment** [6] is ideal for use as an occupational exploration and career development tool. It can also have value in workforce programs looking for a holistic way to assess an individual's occupational interests as well as their potential strengths as an employee.

Based on Howard Gardner's Theory of Multiple Intelligences, this assessment identifies eight distinct intelligences and learning styles. This theory has emerged from recent cognitive research and documents the extent to which students possess different kinds of minds and therefore learn, remember, perform, and understand in different ways.

The Theory of Multiple Intelligences breaks down the eight distinct learning styles:

People Smart: Intrapersonal Intelligence

People who are strong in this area are good at empathizing with others, person-to-person communication, and working in groups. They are skilled at helping others achieve their goals through motivation, teaching, training, counseling, mentoring, and guiding. They typically have many friends, empathy for others, and are street smart. They are best taught through group activities, seminars, and dialogues and learn best through interaction. They benefit from using tools like telephones, audio conferencing, video conferencing, writing, computer conferencing, and email.

Self-Smart: Intrapersonal Intelligence

People who are strong in this area can quickly and easily access and understand feelings, motives, and ideas. They are good at looking inside themselves and overcoming their weaknesses and capitalizing on their strengths. They use information about themselves to make effective decisions. They can understand their own interests, are in tune with their feelings, and tend to shy away from others. They have wisdom, intuition, and motivation as well as a strong will, confidence, and opinions. They can be taught through independent study and introspection and benefit from using tools like books, creative materials, and diaries. They are the most independent of the learners.

Logic Smart or Logical Mathematical Intelligence

People with strong logic and mathematic skills like reasoning and calculating. They think conceptually and abstractly and can see and explore patterns and relationships. They can perform inductive and deductive thinking and reasoning as well as having the ability to understand patterns and relationships. They like to experiment, solve puzzles, and ask cosmic questions. They need to learn and form concepts before they can deal with details. They are good at solving complex analytical problems and experimenting using scientific principles. They are skilled at recognizing and manipulating abstract patterns and relationships and performing mathematical calculations. They are best taught using logic games, investigations, and mysteries.

Picture Smart or Spatial Intelligence

People strong in this area think in terms of physical space. They are very aware of their environments. They like to draw, do jigsaw puzzles, read maps, and daydream. They like to visualize objects and create mental pictures and images. They are strong at seeing and mentally manipulating forms or objects in their mind. They are skilled at creating visual representations of the world, often visualizing the product then working to create that product. They can be taught through drawings and verbal and physical imagery. They benefit from using tools like models, graphics, charts, photographs, drawings, 3D modeling, video, video conferencing, television, multimedia, and texts with pictures/charts/graphs.

Body Smart or Bodily-Kinesthetic Intelligence

People who are strong in this area like to use their body and have a keen sense of body awareness. They like movement and making things. They like to control the physical motion of their own body using fine and gross motor skills. They are good at using their hands to solve problems, create products, or convey emotions and ideas. They are skilled at both physical activities such as sports and fine-motor activities such as arts and crafts. They communicate well through body language and are best taught through physical activity, hands-on learning, acting out, and role playing.

Word Smart: Linguistic Intelligence

Individuals who are strong in this area like to use words effectively. They have highly developed auditory skills and often think in words. They like reading, playing word games, and creating poetry or stories. They have a strong ability to use language through writing and speaking. They are good at using language to convey information as well as to convince, excite, and persuade people. They are skilled at activities that involve reading, writing, listening, and talking. They can best be taught by encouraging them to say and see words, read books, and using computers, games, books, tape recorders, and lectures.

Music Smart: Musical Intelligence

People who are strong in this area have a sensitivity to rhythm, sounds, and tones. They love music and are sensitive to sounds in their environments. They have a good sense of musical pitch and can sing, play musical instruments, and write and compose music. They think in sounds, rhythms, and tonal patterns. They may study better with music in the background. They can be taught by turning lessons into lyrics, speaking rhythmically, and tapping out time using musical instruments, music, and CD-ROMs.

Nature Smart: Naturalist Intelligence

People who are strong in this like the outdoors and have an ability to understand and work effectively in nature and the natural world. They have a strong appreciation for the environment and respect for the beauty of nature. They typically are interested in plants, animals, the environment, and other natural resources. They tend to choose activities such as hiking, camping, hunting, star gazing, swimming, and scuba diving as hobbies (Liptak and Allen 2009).

How to interpret the results

The areas of intelligence where candidates score highest will be a good indicator of the types of jobs and workplace environments where they are best suited. This can be especially helpful for candidates who don't yet have an idea of the type of work they want to do or companies where they'd like to work.

When to administer

Candidates should complete the Work Smarts assessment during the first month of the workshop. If you'd like to assess any changes in a candidate's job preferences, it can be administered again at the end of the workshop.

Where to purchase

Work Smarts is a product of JIST Publishing and can be ordered online using this link.[1] JIST has a full selection of other career exploration products including assessments, videos, workbooks, and books that can also be adapted for use in the workshop.

How do you use a candidate's preferences in exploring possible job options?

Almost all individuals with autism have a clear idea of what they like. From middle and high school and beyond, most know what they would like to do for work. For instance, many enjoy anime so a job at a retail comic book store might be their preference. Some individuals like movies, so a job at a local movie theatre would match their interests. If the individual likes fashion, an internship with a retail clothing store might be a good fit. But a job that requires frequent contact with the public may be too stressful or over-stimulating. A better fit would be as a stock or inventory clerk, any job that has a slower pace and a more predictable work environment. As the candidate shows mastery in these beginning roles, they can be gradually introduced to jobs with more responsibility and interaction with the public.

---

1   http://jist.emcp.com/work-smarts.html

If a candidate is unsure of what they would like to do for work, we help the individual determine their vocational goals using the United States Bureau of Labor Statistics *Occupational Outlook Handbook* (United States Department of Labor, Bureau of Statistics 2015), a comprehensive list of occupations in hundreds of industries with job pay ranges, work experience requirements, and prospective employment outlooks. If required by their job of interest, we help the candidate develop a personalized plan for obtaining training or additional education as required by the job. A workplace readiness training program for middle and high school students must have this as a featured part of their curriculum to help these students make informed decisions on class selections through the end of high school. This is the best way to ensure that these students acquire the skills necessary for a successful transition post high school (United States Department of Labor, Bureau of Statistics 2015).

What workplace paperwork is covered in the workshop?

To help candidates understand the type of paperwork involved when getting a job prepares them to know what to expect when they are hired. Below is the information that we cover in the workshop on Workplace Paperwork.

Social security number

To help candidates understand the importance of a social security number, they need to be instructed of its purpose and reason for keeping the number confidential.

What it is

A social security number is a nine-digit number that is issued to every citizen by the US federal government. It is used to keep track of an individual's lifetime earnings and number of years worked. Upon an individual's retirement or if the individual ever applies for disability or unemployment benefits, the government uses their information to determine their eligibility and calculate their monthly payments. Social Security numbers are also required any time a person files a state or federal tax return or applying for any of the following:

- US passport
- loans
- line of credit
- driver's license
- public assistance.

Importance of confidentiality

A social security number should always be kept as confidential. It should not be carried around unless it is for a specific purpose, like filling out employment paperwork for a new job. The card should always be stored in a safe place at home or in a safe deposit box at a bank. If a card is lost or stolen, the individual will need to apply for a new one from the Social Security Administration.

Employment application

Candidates complete a standard employment application to practice filling one out. A copy of the AWN employment application is included in the last chapter.

W-4

A form W-4 is used by an employer to determine how much federal income tax should be withheld from an employee's paycheck. The IRS recommends that employees submit a new W-4 tax form each year, or any time their personal or financial situation changes.

I-9

Form I-9 is issued by the Department of Homeland Security to verify that a person is legally authorized to work in the United States. Their US employers must have all employees complete a form I-9 when hired. Verification of their employment status requires an employee to present documents that confirm they are eligible to work in the United States. The most common documents used for verification are a state-issued driver's license or ID and a US-issued social security card. A US-issued passport is also common. A copy of the I-9 form is included in the last chapter.

Resume

For an individual with little or no work experience, the best choice is a simple one-page chronological resume that highlights any paid or volunteer work experience, diplomas or certificates received by the student, and their special skills and talents. In lieu of work experience, middle and high school students should also highlight any scholastic awards and community service projects. A resume template is included in the final chapter.

Portfolios

If a student is creative or artistic, a portfolio of their work is essential in demonstrating to employers what they can do. If the student is technologically savvy, a website can be created to display their artwork and musical compositions. The social media site, Pinterest, is an also excellent resource to display a student's artwork and talents.

Chapter 3

Getting Organized with Google

Using Google's Free Apps to Stay Organized,
on Time, and in Communication

*With Google and YouTube, I can pretty much figure out how to
do anything.*

Lacey Brink

The process of finding a job requires many essential life skills, particularly in areas of planning and preparation. To be successful in finding a job, you should know how to locate a job opening, get to your interview on time, dress appropriately, and make a good impression. As discussed in Chapter 1, these skills fall under the term 'executive functioning,' and these are weak for many individuals with autism.

Once hired, many employers expect their workers to be familiar with, or be willing to be trained in, the use of business software like Word, Excel, and PowerPoint. While not all jobs require the use of a computer, candidates with experience with any of these programs can improve their chances of getting hired as well as increase their earnings potential.

How do you help candidates improve their executive functioning skills?

In the Workplace Readiness Workshop, we use Google for its many free apps to help our candidates improve their skills in time management, task completion, and email communication. They also learn how to store important personal information and workshop materials using Google's cloud service. Google also has its own versions of the business software programs Word, Excel, and PowerPoint which we use to create our workshop materials and help our candidates create their resume and other documents. Using a feature on Google called "share," we're able to give our candidates immediate online access to any information presented in class. Since all information is stored in the cloud, candidates may access it at anytime and anywhere using a computer, smartphone, or device with a Wi-Fi connection.

What are the various Google apps used in the Workplace Readiness Workshop?

Google is one of the biggest brands in the world and its search engine is the one of the most popular and widely used—it covers almost 60 percent of the worldwide search engine market. But Google is not just a search engine. There are many free products and services available from Google that are excellent for support in time management, locating addresses, finding directions, estimating time travel, and professional email communication.

Below is a list of Google apps that we use most often in the workshop, how these apps are incorporated into the workshop as an instructional tool, and what executive functions are supporting with each app.

Google search engine

Google's search engine is an essential tool for students, opening a world of knowledge about any topic imaginable. By middle school, most students are extremely experienced at conducting internet research and accessing the web, and almost all students are familiar and regularly use the Google search engine. In the workshop, we utilize the search engine to prepare for field trips by researching the background of the company and the individual that we will be meeting. We also use it to help second year candidates focus on research jobs at potential companies in their communities where they may want to apply.

How Google search engine is incorporated into the workshop

- to conduct internet research for upcoming field trips and job searches

- to research the backgrounds of the field trip hosts that candidates will be meeting and companies where they have interviews.

Work-related executive functions that are supported

- researching, retrieving, and organizing information.

Gmail

Gmail is the most used free email service used by both individuals and companies around the world. Along with email, a Gmail account also gives its user access to a free cloud server as well as other apps that are helpful in strengthening executive functioning skills. A user must be a minimum of 13 years old to open a Google/Gmail account.

If a candidate already has a Gmail address and it is appropriate for use in a business setting, we encourage them to keep using it. Some of our candidates already have Gmail with usernames from their youth (e.g. PennielovesPooh), so we help create a username that is more appropriate for use in a business context. All candidates have an email address by the second class meeting.

How do you choose an email address for a candidate?

The best choice for an email address contains the candidate's first and last name:

jonathansmith@gmail.com

jonathan.smith@gmail.com

If the candidate's first and last name combined is over 12 letters, we use the candidate's first initial and last name:

jsmith@gmail.com

If neither of these email names is available, we use the candidate's first name (or first initial) and last name followed by one, two, or three numbers, whichever is available using the least amount of numbers, for example:

jsmith1@gmail.com

jsmith12@gmail.com (if jsmith1 not available)

jsmith123@gmail.com (if jsmith12 not available)

How Gmail is incorporated into the workshop

- to send emails to candidates, parents, and caregivers about upcoming events
- by candidates to write thank you emails to field trip hosts
- with Google Drive to send emails to candidates with links to workshop materials.

Work-related executive functions that are supported

- composing professional email correspondence
- reviewing emails for spelling and grammar errors
- reviewing workshop information to reinforce concepts taught in class.

Maps

Google Maps lets you view any part of the world in an aerial view or at street level. Maps also has a feature that provides directions to and from an address and travel time between the two destinations.

How Maps is incorporated into the workshop

- to find the locations where upcoming field trips and interviews will take place
- to help candidates estimate time travel for upcoming field trips.

Work-related executive functions that are supported

- finding an address
- planning how to arrive to a location on time
- estimating time travel.

Contacts

Available with Gmail, this feature allows users to store important contact information of friends and business associates.

How Contacts is incorporated into the workshop

- to store contact information for workshop instructors and fellow candidates

- to store information from business cards collected from field trip hosts and when meeting a professional in person.

Work-related executive functions that are supported

- organizing and storing important information for personal and professional contact.

Calendar

This electronic calendar allows users to input events with detailed information including a location or address which links directly to Google Maps. The event can also be shared with anyone with via email, but a word of advice: don't send a Gmail Calendar invitation to a non-Gmail user. There is an incompatibility issue for use with non-Gmail users, and the Calendar email invitation that the person receives will have an incorrect date and time. This is confusing for both you and the invitee and it will require some time on your part to correct.

How Calendar is incorporated into the workshop

- to help candidates to remember workshop events and field trips

- Synced to candidate's smartphones or tablets so they can access their calendar at any time in the community.

Work-related executive functions that are supported

- time and calendar maintenance.

Tasks

This feature allows users to create lists of ongoing tasks and projects. Tasks also has a feature that allows users to assign a project due date that automatically syncs and displays on the user's Google Calendar.

How Tasks is incorporated into the workshop

- to help candidates keep track of any workshop assignments or project due dates.

Work-related executive functions that are supported

- planning and completing projects.

Drive

This app offers free cloud storage service and its own versions of Microsoft's software programs (Word, Excel and PowerPoint). Just like a computer, Drive allows users to name documents and create folders to store information.

Some of our candidates are already familiar with creating word documents, but not as many have experience with spreadsheets or presentations. If a candidate is interested in individualized instruction in any of these programs, community colleges and adult schools are usually good resources for low-cost options.

We use Drive to create all our workshop materials. We also use another program called Forms to create our five-question session review quiz that each candidate completes at the end of each classroom meeting.

How Drive is incorporated into the workshop

- to share workshop materials with candidates
- to help candidates create and store important documents (e.g. resumes or social security cards).

Work-related executive functions that are supported

- organization and creation of important documents.

YouTube

With over 1 billion people visiting each month, YouTube is one of the most popular websites in the world. So, it is no surprise that without exception, all our candidates know and regularly watch videos on

YouTube. With millions of videos posted on the site from people all over the world, YouTube is an incredible resource of information on any subject you can imagine.

How YouTube is incorporated into the workshop
In the workshop, we don't use YouTube as a classroom instructional tool. Instead, we let candidates use it to share videos they enjoy so they can discover any common interests that they share with anyone in the group.

Work-related executive functions that are supported
- sharing information about oneself
- finding common interests with others (Biswal 2016).

Chapter 4

Dress for Success

Knowing What to Wear to Make a Favorable Impression

When I'm dressed for work, I feel ready to work.

Cameron Rosen

For better or worse, we will always be judged by the way we look and the clothes that we wear, so our appearance is an important part of the image we present. First impressions are extremely powerful, and our attire speaks volumes about who we are, the type of work we do, and the lifestyle we lead. And, when we dress sharp, we feel better about ourselves. This helps to boost our self-confidence, which radiates an image of self-worth and self-respect (Devine 2015).

Why is it important to discuss dressing well on the job in a workplace readiness program?

When we go to work, it essential that we match what we wear to the company culture. If we work in the legal or financial industries, we wear a suit to meet the expectations of our boss and clients and to match our attire to what our coworkers are wearing. If we work in a creative field like advertising or fashion, our clothing choices are more individualized and expected to be an expression of our own personal style. Dressing for the job is the first step to fitting in at work, and, to maintain a positive professional image, it's essential that we stick to the style conventions of the culture of the company for which we work.

How important is dress when going for a job interview?

In an interview, your goal is to sell yourself as the best match for the job by answering the interviewer's question, "Why should I hire you?" Dressing well for an interview in a style that matches the company's culture shows that you know how to fit in and are a good match for the organization. If you wear clothes that are ill-fitting, in disrepair, or don't match what everyone else in the company is wearing, you'll most likely be disqualified for the position before you even get to speak, no matter if you are the most qualified candidate and come highly recommended with glowing references.

How do you teach candidates the concept of matching attire to the culture of the company?

Each month, the workshop goes on a community-based field trip which gives our candidates an opportunity to meet face to face with potential employers at their place of business. These visits help our candidates put into practice the skills they're learning in the classroom, which are the skills they need to learn in preparation for an actual interview.

In class, the group spends a good deal of time discussing what each candidate will wear, and if they don't have something appropriate, we help them develop a plan to go shopping to purchase what they will need. We then follow up our discussion with an email to the candidate's parent or caregiver to make sure the candidate can get the help they need to complete this wardrobe task. To further remind candidates of the time and date of their shopping trip, we create and share a Google Calendar event which then appears on each individual candidate's Google calendar. If a candidate needs help from their parent or caregiver, we can share the event with them as well, but only if they have a Gmail account.

How do you teach candidates the importance of wearing clothes that fit properly?

Knowing your correct body measurements is the key to finding clothes that fit well. It's helpful when trying on clothing in a store's fitting room and a necessary part of ordering clothing from an online retailer. To help our candidates understand what size they are in the different types of work clothing, we created two **Measurement Worksheets** [20] (one for men and one for women) where we take the candidate's measurements and record them and then store the information as a Google Doc in the candidate's Google Drive. We then compare their measurements to a standardized US size chart and record their size for shirts, pants, jackets, dresses, skirts, and jackets.

How do you teach candidates about dress variations within a company's culture?

There are occasions where there are variations in the workplace dress code expectations, and it's important to teach candidates what these variations are.

Casual Fridays

In companies with a more conservative style of dress, some have a policy called "casual Friday" where the dress code is relaxed but still professional. It never means to dress too casual so candidates need to understand that it's never alright to wear flip flops, gym clothes, or graphic tee shirts to work.

Staff and client meetings

Usually the same attire worn to the office is appropriate for meetings, but candidates may want to learn that they'll make the best impression when they look their best. For these situations, they may want to put more effort into their clothing choices and pick an outfit that they think looks best on them.

Social events

Candidates need to learn that their clothing selections for events outside the office need to match what is typically worn at similar events. If the event is a company picnic at a park, jeans and a polo shirt with tennis shoes would be acceptable. If the event is the annual company holiday party at an upscale restaurant, men will be expected to wear a business suit or a nice-fitting sports jacket with slacks and women a dress or suit. As is true for typical workplace attire, all candidates' clothing worn to company social outings needs to be clean and in good repair.

How do you provide candidates with additional information on dressing for the workplace?

Our presentation, **Can I Wear this to Work**? shows the differences between formal versus less formal workplace attire and the style of dress suited for various industries. A template of the presentation is included in the final chapter. It can be easily adapted to include photographs for the style of clothing worn for companies and businesses that are a feature of the community where the workshop is being offered.

Do you incorporate social media in classroom instruction?

Pinterest is a visual bookmarking and discovery platform, and its users create "boards" where they "pin" pictures they find online and like and create links to articles and information to share with others. It has more than 100 million monthly active users and offers an endless amount of valuable information on any topic imaginable.

AWN has its own Pinterest page with boards dedicated to each of our monthly topics. This resource is provided to candidates as additional information to supplement what has been covered during class. The boards are full of information, pictures, and articles about wardrobe choices that are appropriate for various industries.

Chapter 5

Interview Essentials

What to Do Before, During and After an Interview

An interview is the first chapter in a story known as your career.

Nicholas Tuso

Being interviewed for a job is a stressful situation for almost everyone. If you're lucky, you've been referred to the job by someone who has spoken highly of your career attributes and stellar work ethic. If you applied for the job through the company's website or answered an ad posted on Craig's List, you may not know the person who you'll be interviewing with or how many other people are also interviewing for the job. From start to finish, the entire job search experience is filled with waiting and anticipation, but planning and preparation can help make it go more smoothly with a better chance of a success in landing your dream job.

What are the biggest fears people have about job interviews?

LaSalle Network, a staffing and recruiting firm headquartered in Chicago, surveyed about 1600 people regarding their feelings about job interviews. Not surprisingly, 81 percent of the respondents reported that they got nervous before an interview, and listed their top fears as saying the wrong thing (50 percent), making a bad impression (44 percent), being unable to sell themselves (36 percent), and being unprepared (28 percent). As Tom Gimble, LaSalle Network Founder and CEO, said, "Being nervous for a job interview is a result of being underprepared. Feeling 'perfectly' prepared isn't enough. People study the statistics of their favorite sports team, they know who the coaches are, the wins vs losses for their favorite teams, the rankings, etcetera. People need to take the same approach when going for a job as they would when studying the details of their hobbies. Nearly all their fears listed in our study are preventable depending on how long a candidate prepares. Preparation trumps nerves" (LaSalle 2015).

What is the most important goal for a job interview?

The main goal in any job interview is to convince the hiring manager that you are the best choice for the job and a good fit for the organization. To get the job, you must make a positive impression upon the interviewer which means wearing the right clothes, asking insightful questions, and presenting a positive self-image. But none of this happens by chance. It requires planning and preparation on the part of interviewees to increase their chance of getting a job.

How do you teach candidates the key steps in preparing for an interview?

Each month, candidates attend a field trip where they meet with professionals at their workplace. In preparation, candidates conduct online research, are assigned questions, instructed on what to wear, determine time travel, and decide on their method of transportation to and from the location. After the field trip, the group composes and sends a group email thanking the field trip host for their time and expressing appreciation on what they learned. The experience provides an excellent opportunity for candidates to generalize the skills they've learned in the classroom in an actual workplace.

Below is a list of skill sets taught in conjunction with our field trips.

Time management

To help candidates understand the concept of time management, AWN created a **Time Management Worksheet** [18] that accounts for everything that is needed to be on time for an appointment. One concept we continually stress is the importance of arriving at least 15 minutes early. To emphasize this point, we use a quote by the great football coach, Vince Lombardi: "If you are five minutes early to an appointment, you are ten minutes late." This 15-minute rule is used for all field trips to reinforce and put into practice this concept.

Research

To accentuate the importance of research in preparation for an interview, the workshop group conducts a Google search on the company and the person that the group will be meeting. This research includes looking at the company's website and reading information about the organization or anything written by the field trip host. Prior to the field trip, candidates are sent an email with links to the information and are assigned homework of reviewing the material on their own outside of class. The practice of checking their Gmail account every day is something that many of our candidates need to be reminded, so this exercise serves twofold: to get our candidates into the habit of checking their Gmail and researching online information about subject they want to learn more about.

Create and assign questions

Instructors conduct their research on the company and create a list of questions. Each candidate is assigned at least one question to ask during the field trip. Candidates are encouraged to come up with their own questions, but we've found that on-the-spot thinking is a challenge for almost all of them. Preparing and assigning questions in advance to each candidate is the good way to help them learn the types of questions that are good to ask during an interview. For each field trip, instructors take notes, transcribe information on a Google Doc, and share the information with each candidate. This document serves as a resource of questions that candidates can use in their own future interviews.

A good night's sleep and a healthy breakfast or lunch

To be their best when meeting our field trip host, we encourage our candidates to get a good night's sleep and have a healthy breakfast or lunch prior to going on the field trip. While the topic of nutrition is not something we go into detail during class instruction, we have a "healthy eating" board on the AWN Pinterest page that provides information on how to maintain a well-balanced diet and incorporate a regular exercise routine into their daily schedule.

Turn your phone off

Nothing can spoil a great meeting more than having a phone ring in the middle of a conversation. We tell our candidates to turn their phone off as soon as they arrive at the field trip location to avoid this mistake.

Stay calm and relaxed

Meeting new people in an unfamiliar environment can be stressful for many people. For individuals with autism, it can be especially stressful. In class, we practice using various stress management techniques like mindful breathing; this is explained in more detail in Chapter 7. If the meeting is something that causes anxiety for a candidate, we suggest practicing stress management techniques prior to arriving at the field trip. For an actual interview, we recommend that candidates practice stress management when they are waiting to meet with their interviewer.

Be positive, smile, and use good manners

Smiling and saying please and thank you are essential to making a good impression. We also tell candidates that when they smile, it comes through in their voice so they should practice this when asking our field trip host a question.

Use a firm handshake

During class, we practice our handshake so candidates know what this should feel like. They are encouraged to practice their handshake with our field trip host.

Get a business card

AWN instructors ask for the host's business card, and this is shared with candidates during the next class meeting to add to their Google contacts.

Send a thank you note

All candidates are advised to follow up every meeting or interview with a thank you email or written note no later than two days afterwards. For field trips, we compose a group thank you email that we send to our host in our next class. By composing the email as a group, we're able to model the appropriate format of a business email.

Is there any additional information that is covered in the workshop during Interview Essentials?

Field trips provide the best opportunity for our candidates to put into practice what they've learned in class, but there is more information about interviews that we do not have an opportunity to practice. Listed below is the information that isn't a part of field trip preparation but is covered in class.

Practice your introduction

To help alleviate the stress associated with an interview, we encourage candidates to practice what they will say when they first meet the company receptionist and when they meet their interviewer. Besides practicing these introductions in class, we encourage our candidates to practice their greetings in front of a mirror so they can see how they appear to others. They are also encouraged to practice their greetings with a trusted adult or friend for their feedback and constructive criticism.

Create a resume

If a candidate doesn't have a resume, we help them create one on Google Docs using the AWN **Resume Worksheet** [10]. Candidates complete the worksheet as a group exercise in class. Those that need extra support can finish it at home with help from a parent or caregiver with the next class meeting as the due date. The Resume Temple is used to show candidates how to properly format a professional resume.

Create an elevator pitch

To help our candidates effectively communicate who they are and the type of job they want, we help them create their own "elevator pitch," a statement from 15 to 60 seconds that quickly and effectively conveys this information to the person they are meeting. If a candidate agrees to be videotaped, we use this as an exercise to provide constructive criticism from other candidates, but if there is any discomfort doing this in front of the group, instructors meet privately to review the tape and provide feedback. The final chapter includes a copy of the **Elevator Pitch Worksheet** [21] that we use to help candidates create their own elevator pitch.

Rehearse answers to commonly asked questions

Candidates are given a list of ten commonly-asked interview questions, and they practice their answers to these questions in class. If a candidate agrees, the exercise is videotaped and viewed for feedback from other candidates or privately with an instructor if the candidate is uncomfortable doing this in front of the group.

Listen to the interviewer's questions

We tell our candidates never to assume anything during an interview. If they don't understand the question, they should ask for an explanation or an example of what the interviewer is thinking. If they don't know the answer to a question, they should not make up an answer or say something that isn't true. Instead, they should admit that they don't know the answer and can offer to get back to the interviewer with an answer after the interview.

Know what to say

Being polite and pleasant during an interview is a must, but equally important is knowing what to say. This includes:

- never saying anything negative about a former job, coworkers, or supervisors

- using appropriate language and never swearing or using slang

- focusing on strengths and transferable skills like enthusiasm for the position and not bringing attention to a lack of experience

- focusing on discussing experience or skills that are directly related to the job

- keeping the discussion on the benefits that the interviewee will bring to the employer and not how the job will benefit the individual.

Follow-up

If a candidate has not heard from the employer by their decision date, we recommend to candidates to call to follow up the day after the decision date. If they reach the person's voice mail, we advise candidates to leave a brief message and to include their phone number.

Learn from the experience

Practice makes perfect, and even if the interview is not a success, we tell candidates that every interview is an opportunity to learn so they can do better in their next interview. To help in this process, AWN created an **Interview Reflection Checklist** [21] to help candidates look back at their interview experience. If the candidate has gone on an interview and is open to discussing their experience with the class, we complete the checklist with the group so all members can also learn from the experience.

What else does the workshop provide to candidates to help them generalize the information about interview preparation?

To help candidates retain the information they've learned in class, AWN created an **Interview Prep Checklist** [21] that outlines the important steps of what to do several days before the interview, what to do during the interview, and how to follow up after the interview. This worksheet is used in conjunction with the **Time Management Worksheet** [18] to help candidates with their time management skills so they arrive to their interview on time.

Chapter 6

Landing a Job

Where to Look, Networking, and Creating a Professional Online Presence

Networking is one of the ways that will further your success in life.

Stephen Gaiber

The saying "You can never have too many friends" was never more true than when it comes to work. As we discussed in Chapter 1, a recommendation from a friend or relative is a key factor in having success in finding a job. Once hired, having friends at our job plays a large part in our level of job satisfaction and a big reason why we stay.

Networking is an important part of any successful job search. Face-to-face meetings with local business owners are a good way to increase your network of professional contacts, which increases your chances for potential job referrals. Job fairs and Chamber of Commerce mixers are excellent places to meet new business contacts. Since these events are geared for adult professionals, middle and high school students should be cleared in advance with the event organizer and attend these events as a group. It's essential that the group has enough adult chaperones to adequately supervise the group until the event ends and the students have gone home.

Another important element of a job search is maintaining a professional social media presence. As a way of highlighting relevant work skills, abilities, and experience, a well-written profile posted on the right social media sites can serve as an effective marketing tool when seeking employment. Many employers routinely review the social media sites when making hiring decisions, so it's important for job seekers to know what's appropriate to post and what not to post on these sites. Some have age restrictions with most requiring users to be a minimum age of 13.

The use of social media by middle and high school students with autism can have many benefits, but it's essential that they are taught how to use it safely and responsibly. Adult supervision in the use of social media for all students needs to be ongoing. Independent use of social media should be allowed only after a student has shown that they are mature enough to use it responsibly.

How do you teach candidates how to network as part of their job search process?

Looking for a job is one of the hardest jobs there is and takes a lot of planning, perseverance, and persistence. It's important to know which companies in your area are hiring and what jobs are available. To know the right people that can refer you to these potential jobs, it's essential to understand how to network to increase the number of your professional contacts.

The following are the ways we recommend to our candidates to help them develop and expand the contacts within their professional network. Candidates should be accompanied to any meetings by a support person to provide help as needed. If a meeting does not go as planned, candidates will need to reflect on the experience to come up with ideas on how they can be more successful in their next meeting. For candidates of all ages including middle and high school students, it is recommended that the person providing these supports isn't a parent or guardian. The activity should be used to help candidates practice their independent work-related life skills. The opportunity to practice these skills independently is lost if the person providing the support is the candidate's primary caregiver.

Talk to the people you know

Because teachers, counselors, and most parents are employed and have their own network of professional contacts, they are an excellent source of referrals for future jobs. To start this process, we help candidates complete a **Google Contact Spreadsheet** [19] in Google Docs listing the names of all the adults they know, their occupations, and their contact information. We also include the names of any friends that are employed. We then help them develop a daily and weekly plan of how they will outreach to these contacts. This schedule is then added to the candidate's Google Task list and a due date is assigned which automatically syncs with the candidate's Google calendar. In preparation of the meeting, we help our candidates develop their "elevator pitch" so they can quickly communicate the type of job they want and ways they can benefit a future employer. Finally, we help our candidates choose who will be helping them to attend the meeting.

Volunteering

Not only is volunteering a good way of giving back to your community, it is also a great way to improve work skills and increase a network of professional contacts. Any work experience, paid or unpaid, looks good on a resume because it shows an employer that the individual has a commitment to work. Even though volunteers do not usually get paid, any volunteer experience can and should be viewed as a way of improving a student's job skills and as a stepping stone to a paying job with additional responsibilities. As Temple Grandin says, the job must be outside the home and have a set schedule.

The best places to start looking for volunteer opportunities are organizations whose missions match the student's likes and passions. Many schools have requirements for service learning hours, and a school's Career Center is a good place for recommendations of available volunteer opportunities. If the experience is a success, students should continue in the position since longevity in any job, either paid or unpaid, looks good to a potential employer.

Internships and temp jobs

Internships provide excellent opportunities to enter the job market and are well suited for middle or high school students if appropriate on-the-job supports are provided. Locating an internship uses the same process as finding a volunteer opportunity. Most internships are unpaid, but some come with a stipend. Temp jobs are an option for students after they leave high school and provide an opportunity to work on a temporary basis before committing to a permanent job. Temp placements are usually handled by an agency who oversees all payroll responsibilities. Unlike permanent employment, temp positions and internships usually last for a specific amount of time.

Attend networking events

Job fairs and Chamber of Commerce mixers are excellent places for candidates to connect to professionals in their field of interest and with business owners in their community. Preparing for these events is the same as preparing for an interview, which provides an opportunity for candidates to put into practice the skills they learned in Interview Essentials. To find information about upcoming job fairs, do a "job fair" Google search for your area. For Chamber of Commerce events in your community, check the website for dates and times of their upcoming mixers and social activities. For middle and high school students, it's important to check in advance with the event organizer for any age restrictions. Students should attend the event as a group with enough adult chaperones to adequately supervise all students until the event's conclusion and each one has gotten a ride home.

Don't forget the business card

Candidates are reminded to always get a business card from any professional they meet and to write down the date and place where the meeting happened. After the meeting, candidates record the information from the business cards into their Google contacts.

What is an informational interview and how can candidates use it in their job search?

An informational interview is an informal conversation with someone working in an area of interest who will give information and advice about their career. It is not a job interview, but it is an opportunity to gain knowledge about a specific occupation. The benefits of informational interviewing include getting firsthand, relevant information about an industry or a specific job, receiving tips on how to prepare and enter a given career, learn what it is like to work for a specific organization, and initiate contact with business professionals (UC Berkeley Career Center 2016).

To help candidates understand the steps required to schedule and conduct an informational interview, AWN has created four worksheets that review what to do before, during, and after the interview meeting (Informational Interview Essentials, Informational Interview Checklist, Informational Interview Scripts & Correspondence, and Informational Interview Worksheet). Our monthly field trips provide our candidates with an excellent opportunity to practice conducting an informational interview in an authentic community-based workplace (Moore Norman Technology Center Employment Services).

How do you help candidates create a professional online presence?

Employers routinely review the social media sites of a prospective employee when making hiring decisions. For this reason, it is important that an individual's online profile contains accurate and updated information about relevant job skills and experience that is consistent across all social media sites.

A candidate's social media presence is not just their personal outlet; it is also their brand that identifies who they are, what they like to do, and the type of activities they like to participate in. For this important reason, candidates must never post anything that could be viewed negatively by potential employers. They should also use their social media privacy settings to control what's posted on their social media profiles. Rosemary Haefner, Vice President of Human Resources at CareerBuilder says:

> It's important for job seekers to remember that much of what they post on the Internet—and in some cases what others post about them—can be found by potential employers, and that can affect their chances of getting hired down the road… Job seekers need to stay vigilant and pay attention to privacy updates on all of their social networking accounts so they know what information about them is out there for others to see. Take control of your web presence by limiting who can post to your profile and monitoring posts you've been tagged in. (CareerBuilder 2014)

In creating an online profile, we encourage candidates to review the profiles of professionals that they know to see what they are wearing in their profile picture and how their profile is formatted. For middle and high school students that have limited work experience, it's important that they highlight information about their school projects, club memberships, and any special recognition and awards they've received. These include blogs to which they regularly contribute, honor roll awards, and competition medals. To be sure that their profile picture looks professional, we remind students to practice proper hygiene before taking their picture, which includes having clean hair with a recent haircut and, for male students, to be clean shaven.

What professional and personal social media sites do you recommend to candidates?

To help extend their online presence we assist candidates in creating profiles on various social media websites. Although personal social media sites might not seem as important as the business sites, some employers also check these before making a hiring decision, so we encourage our candidates to maintain profiles on the most popular ones. These sites are also good places for candidates to connect with coworkers away from the office, which can help in development of meaningful work friendships.

To help them understand how to use social media responsibly, candidates of all ages must be taught how to use it properly. They must learn the consequence of posting offensive or inappropriate comments, pictures, and materials. This is especially important for individuals with autism who may fail to understand appropriate social cues or have challenges comprehending the consequences of their actions.

It's important that candidates understand the consequences for abusing social media. Middle and high school students probably already know that it can result in a bad reputation with teachers and fellow students or maybe even get them suspended or expelled if the offense is serious. For work, an inappropriate social media post could cost them a potential job, negatively affect the relationship with coworkers, or, if their post is extremely offensive, get them fired. It's also essential that they learn how use social media safely. This includes never giving out their personal information to anyone they meet online or meeting anyone in person that they've only met through social media.

Which social media sites do you recommend for your candidates?

The sites listed below are offered at no cost to the users, although some charge fees for their premium services. Age restrictions apply for each of these sites.

Personal websites

Some students may already be regular users of social media. Especially for any middle and high school students, it is highly recommended that a parent or guardian monitor what their child does on social media to ensure that it is being used safely and responsibly until their child shows they are mature enough to use it on their own. The minimum age requirement for these three sites is 13 years.

Facebook

This is one of the most popular social sites with over 1.79 billion active monthly users from around the world. When users become friends with other users, they can view what they post and share articles, photos, and videos. Facebook does not offer services for job seekers, but users can include information on their profile about their work history and educational background.

Twitter

This is a news and social networking service where users can post 140-character messages called "tweets." It has over 313 million active users and is popular with many celebrities, politicians, and social activists. In addition to posting tweets, users can "follow" other users to view their tweets. Like Facebook, Twitter does not offer services for job seekers, but users can create a profile that includes a brief description about themselves.

Pinterest

This is a photo-sharing website where users can upload, save, sort, and manage images, known as "pins", and other media content, which can be organized into folders sorted by a central topic or theme. Users can follow other users on Pinterest and browse the content of their feeds. If a candidate is creative or has a special talent or skill, a Pinterest page can be used as an online portfolio to display their artwork and projects. AWN has its own Pinterest page and uses it to compile information about all the topics that are covered in class. This is provided to candidates as a supplemental work information resource that they can access at any time.

Business websites

These sites are geared towards working professionals, but it is a good idea to introduce these resources to middle and high school students for their future job search needs. Just as is recommended for personal social media, the use of these sites by students should be monitored by a parent or guardian to ensure that the student is using each one safely and responsibly. Age limits for each of these sites apply.

Monster and CareerBuilder

These are of two of the most visited employment websites in the US and around the world. Both sites allow users to search their job listings and company profiles and post online resumes. They also allow users to sign up for their online, career-advice newsletter and offer free services like resume critiques. *The minimum age requirement for both sites is 13.*

LinkedIn

This is a business, and employment-oriented social networking service with more than 467 million members including more than 40 million students and recent graduates in over 200 countries and territories. LinkedIn users can search their job listings, post a professional profile, and view information about potential employers. LinkedIn also allows users to post updates about their activities, share information and articles with other LinkedIn users, and join "groups" that are focused on specific interests and topics. *The minimum age requirement is 18.*

Indeed

This is a worldwide employment-related search engine of job listings that are aggregated from thousands of websites, job boards, staffing firms, associations, and company career pages. The site allows users to search their listings for available job openings and to post their resume online. *The minimum age requirement is 14 and adult supervision is required for users under 18.*

What other online resources are there to search for employment?

Craigslist is an online resource for almost anything you can imagine, with sites all over the country and around the world. There is a large job listing section that includes a large variety of job postings from entry level to senior management. Many employers use the site to advertise job openings since the cost to post an ad is only $25. Some of the Craigslist sections on each site are appropriate for adults only, so it is highly recommended that a parent or guardian monitor their child's use of these sites.

What is the biggest difference between having a personal job referral and applying for a job posted online?

As discussed, a personal referral is always the most reliable way to find a job. If you have been referred for a job, there may be only a few people in consideration for the position. Once a job has been posted online, it can be viewed by hundreds and maybe thousands of people besides yourself, so anytime you apply for a job in response to an online job posting you will be competing against many people for the same job. For this reason, it is common not to receive a response to an online job inquiry even if you've written an excellent cover letter and are well qualified for the position.

What other employment services are available to individuals with autism?

Every state in the US has a Department of Vocational Rehabilitation (or DOR) Services which offers a variety of employment services to individuals with disabilities including direct job placements and job training. Like the IEP, which is created to help the students accomplish their academic goals, the DOR develops an Individual Plan for Employment (IPE) for each of their clients to identify employment goals and develop a plan of supports to accomplish those goals.

DOR services are available to individuals after high school, so students must be within six months of obtaining their diploma or certificate of completion before they can open a case. If a student is interested in pursuing services with DOR, AWN provides an information sheet with the address of the office closest to where the candidate lives, a listing of the documents that they need to bring to their meeting, and an overview of the process that is involved in opening their case. If a candidate needs help with transportation and someone to accompany them to the meeting, we help them identify who this will be and coordinate getting the information about the meeting to that person. If it can be coordinated, a field trip for high school students to the local DOR office would be a good learning experience to help them understand the process of applying for services.

Chapter 7

Connecting and coworkers

Maintaining Positive Workplace Relationships On and Off the Job

Having friends is one of the most important things in life.

Chris Grayson

Positive social connections have a direct impact on our health and wellbeing. Research has shown that social isolation and lack of social support can have a direct link to an increased risk of various disease outcomes and reduced length of life (House, Landis, and Umberson 1988). Social relationships in the workplace are equally important. A friend on the job can let you in on the inner workings of your office, make the job more enjoyable, and can even enhance your creativity and productivity (Yager 1999).

How are social communication skills affected in individuals with autism?

As we discussed in Chapter 1, children with autism benefit greatly from an early intervention program that includes supports tailored to their specific needs, but, even with supports, some of these children have a tough time transitioning into adolescence. In fact, studies have shown that as children with autism age, their challenges can worsen. A study of 185 individuals with autism from ages 5 to 18 years showed the greatest problems in the youngest and oldest cohorts (Rosenthal *et al.* 2013). A study of 120 individuals with autism who were diagnosed in childhood and re-evaluated again at ages 17 to 40 showed an overall poor outcome in 78 percent of cases (Billstedt, Gillberg and Gillberg 2005).

How do you teach candidates appropriate workplace social communication skills?

Social communication is dynamic and fluid and is influenced by the context in which it occurs. A conversation is an experience that happens spontaneously and can't be scripted or planned. For the conversation to flow, participants must listen to one another, process what is being said, and formulate a response. A conversation is much like a ping pong game where the objective is to keep the ball bouncing between two paddles. In a conversation, responses bounce between participants until the conversation ends.

The first half of the workshop is the Roundtable Discussion, and its purpose is to simulate a workplace setting like a break room. During this part of the workshop, candidates sit around a table and share information about themselves. They also practice recalling information that they learned about other candidates. Sharing information tends not to be too difficult, but remembering information about others is usually not so easy. This can pose a problem in the workplace since our coworkers expect us to remember the information that they've shared and for us to ask about it the next time we see one another.

In our workshop, we use several exercises to help candidates improve their conversational skills.

Sharing information about their week: Each week, candidates share aloud with the group what they did during their week. To help them develop their narrative, AWN created a **Your Week Worksheet—What Happened with You?** [11] that asks questions about the who, what, when, where, and favorite part of their activities. Candidates then go around the table and share with the group the highlights of their week.

Remembering information about others: For the first month, candidates share information about themselves. After a month into the program, candidates are paired and then each one interviews the other using the **Your Week Worksheet—Interview your Partner** [11] to create a narrative of their partner's week. Candidates then go around the table and share their information with the group. Another opportunity where candidates practice workplace communication skills is during our monthly friend trip visiting professionals in their place of business. During the meeting, our candidates ask questions and engage in one-on-one conversations with the field trip host.

Icebreakers: At the beginning of most classes, candidates answer an "Icebreaker" question. Questions are typically about their favorite things like pets, movies, vacations, and restaurants. Their answers are recorded on the **Icebreaker Worksheet** [12] in Google Docs which is then shared with all candidates. The purpose of this activity is to help candidates share information about themselves and learn about members of the group. These questions are all on topics that are appropriate to discuss at work, so the exercise helps candidates learn about what they can ask of their coworkers to get to know them better. A list of icebreaker questions is included in the final chapter.

Planned social activities: Planned outings provide an excellent opportunity for candidates to practice their conversational skills. After some field trips, AWN coordinates a place where candidates and the person who provided transportation (usually a parent) can meet to share a meal. These settings are the types of places where coworkers socialize outside the office and, since these are also attended by workshop instructors, provide an opportunity to gauge how well candidates are generalizing their conversational skills.

Another opportunity where candidates practice their communication skills is during AWN-organized parties. During the holiday season, AWN organizes at least one get-together and invites all candidates and their families. July 4th and Memorial Day weekend are also good times to organize a group get-together. These events are pot luck, which is a common practice for many office parties. For candidates, it's a fun shared experience much like it is for the employees who attend their company's annual holiday party.

For a group of middle and high school students, planning a group party provides an excellent opportunity to practice many organizational and communication skills that are applicable in the workplace. If possible, it's recommended that the group coordinates with the parents of one the students to hold a potluck party in one of their homes on a weekend afternoon or evening. This event would provide students with an opportunity to socialize outside of school and for parents and guardians to get to know one another. If any student requires support during the party, make sure to have a responsible adult on hand and let students know that this support is available if needed. If a student has an in-class aide, consider inviting the aide as a guest but first check with your school to see if this is allowed. If you want the aide to help the student during the party, you will need to check with your school, and, if it is allowed, be sure to agree before the party how many hours the aide will be needed. Also, remember to compensate the aide for the hours worked.

How do you teach candidates the importance of making a good first impression at work?

As the saying goes, "You never get a second chance to make a first impression," and research has shown this to be true. The results of one study showed that social judgments made from viewing faces are formulated rapidly without much mental effort (Bar, Neta, and Linz, 2006; Willis and Todorov 2006). The results from other studies show that social judgments from faces predict important social outcomes ranging from sentencing decisions to electoral success (Blair, Judd, and Chapleau, 2004; Eberhardt *et al.* 2006; Little *et al.* 2007; Montepare and Zebrowitz, 1998; Zebrowitz and McDonald, 1991).

But how long does it take to make a first impression? According to Princeton psychologists Janine Willis and Alexander Todoroc, not much time at all. These researchers found it only took a tenth of a second to form an impression of a stranger after looking at their face. Longer exposures didn't significantly alter those judgments. It only helped the observer to become more confident in their initial judgment (Willis and Todorov 2006).

Because making good first impressions is so important, we help candidates practice ways to do this. Our handout **Making a Good First Impression** is used to help our candidates understand the basics of making and maintaining positive connections with coworkers and supervisors (Americas Job Exchange).

How important is it for candidates to socialize with coworkers outside the workplace?

The workplace provides us with an opportunity to meet people, but we bond as friends during breaks, after work, and on weekends. But before these opportunities to socialize can materialize, we must make a good impression on our coworkers so they will want to get to know us better and spend time with us outside the work.

For middle and high school students, socializing with fellow candidates and making social connections on the job will probably be an area where they need significant support. An in-class aide or job coach can model appropriate behaviors that can help the student make a good impression and form positive connections to their fellow students in class. Eventually, these connections will need to be made with coworkers on the job. If a social situation did not go as planned, it's essential that the support person helps the student reflect on what occurred and problem solve on what could be done differently in a similar situation in the future.

If a middle or high school student is working and makes plans to socialize with a coworker outside the office, it is highly recommended that a responsible adult accompanies the student on the activity. The most important reason is to ensure the student's safety, but if needed, the chaperone can help facilitate positive communication and help the student problem solve after the event if anything doesn't go as planned. It is ideal for the chaperone to be close in age to the student and not the student's parent or guardian.

In relationship to work, why is it important to teach stress management to individuals with autism?

Studies have shown that children with autism have more severe symptoms of social phobias than other groups of children. Adolescents with the diagnosis of high functioning autism are even more likely to have a comorbid diagnosis of an anxiety disorder. One theory is that teenagers with high cognitive functioning are more aware of their environment and the way that they are viewed by others, and this becomes more pronounced as they enter adolescence (Alfano, Beidel and Turner 2006).

In the workplace, it is essential that employees have strategies to self-regulate so they can proactively manage their stress without negatively affecting the work environment. If they have a meltdown at work, they can disrupt the entire workplace. If they are anxious about meeting new people, it can impede their ability to form meaningful relationships with their coworkers. If they are obsessed about something that happened the night before, they will have a hard time staying focused and completing their work tasks.

Proactive stress management techniques are an effective strategy in helping adolescents and adults take control of their emotions so their emotions don't take control over them. During the Roundtable Discussion, we address the topic of stress management by helping candidates identify their physical sensations of stress as well as teaching and practicing proactive strategies that will help with managing their stress levels. Below are the strategies that we use with our candidates to help them accomplish this goal.

The Incredible 5-Point Scale

To assess the consequences of our actions, we must be able to determine how to act, react, and interact in each situation, but to do this, we must be self-aware and able to self-regulate. For individuals with autism, these abilities are impacted to varying degrees. The Incredible 5-Point Scale was developed by Kari Dunn Buron and Mitzi Curtis to help the students with autism understand how to match their emotional response to the appropriate social interaction. Using a number rating system, students can identify their feelings in response to a situation to assess what their expected response to that situation should be (Buron and Curtis 2003). The 5-Point Scale is also an effective technique to use with adolescents and adults with autism to manage their stress.

We begin each workshop by using a 5-Point Scale that has been adapted by AWN. We use it to help candidates self-identify their feelings. They then they go around room and share which number on the scale corresponds to how they are feeling. This exercise is also a useful tool for instructors to gauge how motivated each candidate will be to participate in the workshop.

Below is the rating scale used in the **AWN Incredible 5-Point Group Check in Scale** [13]. As shown, we also match a color to each number/rating:

1 (Blue): I am glad to be here. I will participate and I may even be able to help others.

2 (Green): I am glad to be here and I will participate.

3 (Yellow): I'm here. I might or might not participate.

4 (Orange): I'm here. I will not participate but I will not disrupt.

5 (Red): I will not participate and I may disrupt if I should stay.

To help candidates learn how to independently implement the 5-Point Scale, we have them match a level 1 to how they feel when they are doing something they love, which for our candidates are things like going to Disneyland, seeing a movie, or shopping for Anime. At level 2 they are still feeling good but less excited than they are at a level 1. Both levels are both appropriate for the workplace. At a level 3, they are starting to feel bothered, frustrated, or annoyed. When they experience these feelings, we advise our candidates to stop, take a break, and use a stress management technique so they can return to a level 1 or 2.

The AWN Incredible 5-Point Stress Meter is used to help Candidates match their facial expressions to their feels for each point in the scale and would look something like this:

1. Happy face with big smile

2. Happy face with smaller smiler

3. Face with a worried look

4. Angry face

5. Very angry face

SODA: Stop, Observe, Deliberate, Act

The social behavioral strategy, SODA, was developed by Majorie Bock to address the Theory of Mind impairments for children with autism. Its purpose is to help them stop and reflect before deciding how they will react in a social situation (Bock 2001). It is also an effective strategy for use with adolescents and adults with autism in workplace settings. By helping them to stop and think before acting, candidates can use SODA to avoid making careless mistakes at work and help them consider alternate perspectives of their coworkers and supervisors.

The four components of SODA are:

1. Stop: allows the individual to stop and see what others are doing

2. Observe: helps the individual note what social cues are being used by people in that setting

3. Deliberate: encourages the individual to consider how they are being perceived by others and think about what they might say or do

4. Act: Based on this information, the individual makes a choice on how they will interact.

Mindfulness awareness

Mindful awareness can be defined as paying attention to present moment experiences with openness, curiosity, and a willingness to be with what is. It invites us to stop, breathe, observe, and connect with our inner experience. There are many ways to bring mindfulness into our lives, such as meditation, yoga, art, or time in nature. Mindfulness can be implemented in daily life, by people of any age, profession, or background. In the last ten years, significant research has shown that mindfulness can effectively address health issues to lower blood pressure, boost the immune system, increase attention and focus in ADHD, and lower anxiety and depression. It can foster well-being and less emotional reactivity and thicken the brain in areas in charge of decision making, emotional flexibility, and empathy (UCLA Mindful Awareness Research Center 2016).

To help our candidates understand the concept of mindfulness, AWN created a one-page write-up of the steps used in a mindfulness breathing exercise. During the Roundtable Discussion, we practice the mindfulness breathing activity with our candidates, usually during the first class of the month. To help it to become a habit, we encourage our candidates to practice the mindful breathing each day for a minimum of three to five minutes.

Free resource: UCLA Mindfulness Awareness Research Center

The Mindful Awareness Research Center (MARC) is located at the University of California, Los Angeles that was founded by internationally acclaimed author, educator, and child psychiatrist, Daniel J. Siegel, M.D. MARC's mission is to foster mindful awareness across the lifespan through education and research as well as to promote well-being and a more compassionate society. It offers classes and workshops to the public and provides mindfulness tools and classes to mental health professionals. MARC's website has a page with eight free guided meditations that are also available on iTunes.[1]

AWN Stress Management Worksheet

Self-reflection is an effective tool to monitor one's behavior and general state of mind in a situation. For individuals with autism, it can be an especially effective tool in helping them better understand their actions and to come up with more effective ways in which they can handle a stressful situation in the future.

To help our candidates self-reflect on how they reacted to a stressful situation, AWN created a **Stress Management Worksheet** [17] designed to help record the specifics of an incident and the candidate's bodily reactions. The worksheet is most effective if used immediately after an incident while the details are still fresh, and we recommend that candidates receive support from a responsible adult to complete the worksheet. If the situation did not go as planned, candidates need help to problem solve on ways they might react differently in the future. For this activity, while it is not ideal, it is okay for a candidate to receive help from a parent or guardian.

Why is it important for candidates to learn about the organizational structure of the company where they work?

Understanding an organization's structure helps an employee understand how their job fits within the organization and who at their company is responsible for making business decisions. A well-defined organizational structure improves a company's operational efficiency

---

1   http://marc.ucla.edu/mindful-meditations

because it helps different departments work more smoothly together to focus their time and energy on completing productive tasks. A company's organizational structure can also provide an easily understood track for employees to advance within the ranks of the organization (Ingram 2016).

As we discussed in Chapter 1, to find meaning in our work, it's important to know how our work fits within the larger context of the company. We need to know the jobs that are performed by our coworkers and how their work relates to what we do. It's also important to know the names of the company's managers and senior managers and their role within the company. Understanding an organization's structure and hierarchy of employees is easy if the company has a small number of workers. It becomes more difficult when the company is large with many departments and employees and multiple layers of management.

It's important that candidates learn about the structure of the company for which they work as soon as they are hired so they can understand which employees are at their level as well as the hierarchy of the company's managers and senior management. Candidates also need to learn how their social interaction with coworkers is different than their interactions with their supervisors and people that are higher up in the company. Since most candidates are not yet employed, the best way to teach appropriate social interactions with supervisors and senior management is to role play different scenarios that could happen in the workplace.

For middle and high school students, creating an organizational chart for their school can help them understand the concept of the hierarchy of employees in a company. Ask the principal for a copy of the school's organizational chart or create one yourself. It should list the succession of employees starting with the School District Board of Directors at the top with aides at the bottom. Figure 7.1 gives an example of what school's organizational chart might look like.

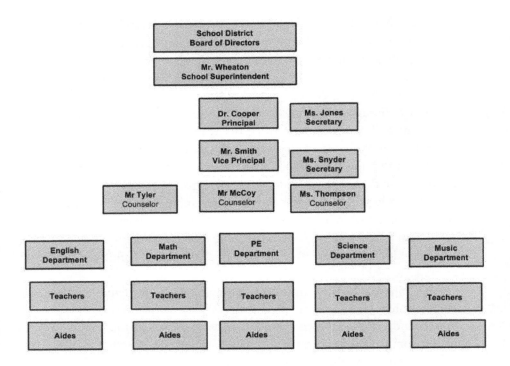

Figure 7.1 ABS High School Organizational Chart

Chapter 8

Understanding the Workplace

Know Your Rights and Effective Self-Advocacy

When I know what the rules are, it's easier to do my job.

Zachary Picard

The time you've spent planning and preparing has finally paid off. You've aced the interview and you've been hired. You have the technical skills that you need to get the job done. You've improved your soft skills so you can get along with your coworkers and handle the responsibilities of your job. What more do you need? To understand your legal protections as an employee, it's important to know the state and federal labor laws that protect you from unfair treatment by your employer and your coworkers.

If you are a worker with a disability, it's also important to be familiar with the Americans with Disabilities Act to know about regulations that shield you from discrimination as well as the types of accommodations to which you are entitled. Since these accommodations are only available to you if you disclose your disability to your employer, you also need to know how and to whom you should disclose. To understand who this is, it's necessary to know the hierarchy of the jobs within your organization and the essential role of your company's human resources department.

To maintain a happy workplace, employees need to know how to respectfully and amicably resolve conflicts. This requires the ability to empathize with another person's viewpoint, but understanding the thoughts and feelings of others tends to be a challenge for many individuals on the autism spectrum. To help our candidates learn how to effectively resolve conflicts, we use the Interest-Based Relational (IBR) approach which provides an easy to follow, step-by-step conflict resolution technique that is easily adapted for use in the workplace.

How do you teach candidates about the hierarchy of jobs within an organization?

As we discussed in Chapter 1, to find meaning in the work that we do, it's important that we understand how our daily tasks are connected to the mission of the company for which we work. To help our candidates understand this concept, we break down the structure of a company into four levels.

> **Level 1—Management Employees:** This group makes plans for the company's growth and manages the work of lower level employees. They have a vast amount of knowledge and years of experience in their field. This level has employees with job titles like Chief Executive Officer (CEO), Chief Operating Officer (COO), and General Manager.

> **Level 2—Executive Employees:** This group has supervisory duties and these employees are usually the representatives for the company when dealing with the public. They have specialization in their field and work with team members to grow their department within the company. This level has employees with job titles like Executive Director, Chief Technical Officer, Chief Financial Officer, President, Vice President, Community Relations Manager, Treasurer, and Assistant Manager.

> **Level 3—Entry Level Employees:** This group does not usually have any authority to make business decisions and workers mainly support the work of the organization's management and executive employees. They mostly work on a fixed schedule and perform work that is assigned to them. This level includes employees with job titles like Clerk, Cashier, Administrative Assistant, Sales Associate, Stock Clerk, Trainee, and Intern.

> **Level 4—Non-Administrative Employees:** The employees in this group have jobs that require physical strength and the performance of some type of manual labor. They typically have a daily work schedule and may be skilled in a specific trade. This level

includes employees with job titles like Security Guard, Custodian, Gardener, Foreman, and Maintenance Worker (Locsin n.d.).

What information is covered about the role of a human resources department?

Human resources (commonly known as HR) is responsible for employee relations and finding candidates to fill job openings. HR conducts interviews, handles the hiring and firing of employees, and completes the necessary paperwork for new hires and exiting employees. HR oversees all matters covering payroll, insurance, benefits, and taxes, and stays up to date on all legal matters affecting employment. HR provides employees with information about assistance programs and is the place where employees can go to ask questions and lodge complaints. When needed, HR provides counseling and mediation to resolve issues within the company.

It's important for candidates to know the function of an organization's HR department and how they can use it help manage conflicts or problems at work. When hired for a new job, candidates are instructed to get the HR person's business card and enter the information into their Google Contacts (Reference.com 2017).

Which state and federal employment regulations are covered in the workshop?

There are literally hundreds of state and federal laws that cover workers in all fifty states. While it is impossible for someone that is not an HR professional to be familiar with every single one, there are a few that all employees should know and understand. Federal laws apply to employees in all 50 states, but state-mandated regulations apply to workers only in the state where they've been enacted. When creating instructional materials for this portion of the workshop, the curriculum needs to be adapted to the labor laws for the state where the program is being offered.

Employment labor law, also referred to as labor law, governs the rights and duties between employers and workers. These rules are primarily in place to protect workers' rights to ensure that they are treated fairly, but there are laws that protect an employer's interests as well. Employment laws are based on federal and state constitutions, legislation, administrative rules, and court opinions. An employment relationship may also be governed by contract (HG.org 2017).

Employment contracts

An employment contract is a legally binding agreement between an employer and an employee regarding a term of employment. The agreement can be oral, written, or implied. We instruct candidates before they start a new job to get a letter from their employer that confirms their rate of pay, employment status, and start date.

At-will employment

Most employees in the United States are presumed to be working at will. This means that the employee can quit or be fired at any time for any reason that isn't illegal under state and federal laws. An employee cannot legally be fired for exercising their rights. This includes using family and medical leave, leave to serve in the military, or taking time off to vote. If an at-will employee is fired, it is the responsibility of the employer to prove "just cause" for the termination (Guerin 2017).

Independent contractors

People who are self-employed in an independent trade, business, or profession in which they offer their services to the public are considered independent contractors. Independent contractors that earn more than $400 in a year must pay quarterly self-employment (SE) taxes based on their income. SE taxes are like the social security and Medicare taxes paid by employed workers. For any candidate that plans to start their own business, it is essential that they understand their responsibility to set aside money from their earnings so they can pay their quarterly SE taxes on a timely basis or be subject to IRS-imposed fines and penalties (United States Internal Revenue Service 2016b).

Exempt vs nonexempt

These are the two classifications of employees as determined the Fair Labor Standards Act (FLSA) which covers rules for employees covering minimum wage requirements, overtime pay, and other protections.

Exempt employees are excluded from all FLSA rules. These are typically employees in executive, supervisory, professional, and outside sales jobs that draw a set salary and have a work schedule with varying hours. Nonexempt employees are typically paid an hourly salary, have a set work schedule, and are covered under FLSA regulations. Rules covering safe and healthy workplace environments, equal employment opportunities, and the rights provided under the Family and Medical Leave Act apply to both exempt and nonexempt employees. Most of our candidates and almost all middle and high school students will be hired as a nonexempt employee for their first job. Still, it's important that they understand the difference between the status as an exempt and nonexempt employee if they are ever hired in an executive or supervisory role (Monster 2017).

Payroll taxes

Especially for middle and high school students that have limited or no work experience, it's important that they understand that when they receive their paycheck, it won't be for the full amount of their hourly wages. Their employer will be withholding a percentage of their check to cover state and federal taxes. To help our candidates understand the reason for these deductions, it's important to provide an overview of what these are.

Federal income tax

Employers generally withhold federal income tax from an employee's wages. Upon being hired, a form W-4 is completed by the employee and this information is used to determine the amount of federal income tax that is withheld from each paycheck. Workers that make over $400 in a year must report their earnings to the Internal Revenue Service (commonly known as IRS) each year by April 15.

State income tax

In all but ten states (Alaska, Florida, Nevada, New Hampshire, South Dakota, Tennessee, Texas, Washington, and Wyoming), workers are required to pay an annual state income tax that is due on April 15 of each year.

Social security and Medicare taxes

Employers also deduct social security and Medicare taxes from each employee's paycheck.

How these taxes are paid

It is the responsibility of the employer to deposit all money deducted from the checks of their employees into an account with an authorized bank or financial institution pursuant to Federal Tax Deposit Requirements. The employer must file an annual return reporting the money that was collected and transfer these funds to the IRS on a timely basis (United States Internal Revenue Service 2016a).

State laws

As mentioned, state regulations vary from state to state, so the information in this portion of the workshop must be matched to the laws of the state where the program is being offered. The regulations that are most important for candidates to be familiar with are:

- state minimum wage rates (if these differ from federal regulations)
- minimum paid rest periods
- minimum meal perils
- payday requirements.

The United States Department of Labor website has the most recent information about the labor laws for each state (United States Department of Labor, Wage and Hour Division n.d).

Employment benefits

State unemployment insurance benefits

The Federal-State Unemployment Insurance Program provides temporary financial benefits to unemployed workers. Each state administers its own program within guidelines established by federal law. Benefit amounts are based on a percentage of an individual's earnings over a recent 52-week period up to a maximum amount established by the state for up to 26 weeks. The funding for the program in most states is provided by a tax imposed on employers. Benefits paid to recipients must be reported on a federal income tax return (United States Department of Labor n.d).

The United States Department of Labor website has the most recent information about the Unemployment Program for each state

(United States Department of Labor, Employment & Training Administration 2015b).

Worker's compensation

Workers' compensation (also known as workman's comp) is a state-mandated insurance program that provides financial benefits to employees who suffer job-related injuries and illnesses. The federal government administers the program which provides replacement benefits, medical treatment, vocational rehabilitation, and other benefits, but each state establishes the rules and regulations for the workman's comp program in their state. In general, an employee with a work-related illness or injury can get workman's comp benefits regardless of who was at fault. In exchange for these guaranteed benefits, employees usually do not have the right to sue their employer in court for damages they've incurred due to their injuries (Nolo 2017).

The United States Department of Labor website has the most recent information about the Workers' Compensation program in your state: (United States Department of Labor, Office of Workers' Compensation Programs n.d.).

Federal laws

In the United States, the United States Department of Labor administers and enforces federal laws covering workplace activities for about 10 million employers and 125 million workers. Below is a description of the laws most commonly applicable to job seekers and workers. Candidates are instructed to see their human resources manager if they feel that their employer is in violation of any of these laws or if they would like to take advantage of any of the federal or state employment benefits to which they are entitled.

Wage and hours

The Fair Labor Standards Act (FLSA) sets the standard for wages and is administered by the Wage and Hour Division (WHD) of the US Department of Labor. For a state or city that has enacted laws setting a higher hourly minimum wage, the higher rate would apply to all workers in that city or state. The Act establishes overtime pay of one-and-one-half times the regular rate of pay when an employee works over 40 hours in one week, but there are no overtime pay requirements for hours worked on weekends or holidays unless the employee has exceeded working 40 hours. The FLSA establishes 14 years of age as the minimum age for employment, limits the number of hours that children under the age of 16 can work, and forbids the employment of children under the age of 18 for jobs deemed too dangerous. The WHD also enforces the labor standard provisions of the Immigration and Nationality Act that applies to aliens working in the under certain immigrant visa programs. The current federal minimum wage standard is $7.25 (United States Department of Labor n.d.).

The most convenient link to determine your state's minimum wage standard is from the United States Department of Labor on Minimum Wage Laws in States (United States Department of Labor, Wage and Hour Division 2017).

Family and Medical Leave Act (FMLA)

Administered by the WHD, the FMLA requires employers of 50 or more employees to give up to 12 weeks of unpaid, job-protected leave to eligible employees for the birth or adoption of a child or for the serious illness of the employee or a spouse, child, or parent. The link on the FMLA is an excellent resource to review the information during class when discussing this topic (United States Department of Labor, Wage and Hour Division 2015a).

Workplace safety and health

The Occupational Safety and Health (OSH) Act is administered by the Occupational Safety and Health Administration (OSHA). It covers safety and health conditions for most private-sector and all public-sector employees to guarantee employees a workplace free from recognized, serious hazards (United States Department of Labor, Occupational Safety and Health Administration 2004).

Whistleblower and retaliation protections

OSHA administers the "whistleblower" protection provisions of twenty-two states. Under this law, an employee may file a complaint with OSHA if they believe that they have received discrimination or retaliation for exercising any right afforded by OSH. An employee must file a complaint about any health or safety issues within 30 days after the occurrence of the alleged violation (United States Department of Labor).

Worker Adjustment and Retraining Notification Act (WARN)

This federal law mandates that workers being laid off be given a written 60 day notice before the date of mass layoffs or plant closings. A worker that does not receive notice per the law may seek damages for back pay and benefits for up to 60 days depending on how many days' notice were received (US Department of Labor, Employment and Training Administration Fact Sheet 1989).

Harassment

Harassment in the workplace based on race, color, religion, sex, national origin, age, and disability in any form is prohibited by law. It becomes unlawful when the offensive conduct becomes a condition of continued employment or the conduct is severe or pervasive enough to create a work environment that a reasonable person would consider intimidating, hostile, or abusive. An employer is automatically held liable for harassment by a supervisor that results in a negative employment action such as termination, failure to promote, or be hired. An employer is also held liable if it was known or should have been known about the harassment and he failed to take prompt and appropriate corrective action. The Equal Employment Opportunity Commission (or EEOC) handles administration and enforcement of laws covering harassment (U.S. Equal Employment Opportunity Commission n.d.b).

When offering a workshop to middle and high school students, the topic of harassment might be one that they're familiar. They may have been bullied at one time or could currently be the target of bullying behavior at school or elsewhere. Especially if the group has bonded and formed any sort of connection, the workshop may become a safe environment for these students, a place where they can share their experiences and their feelings without being judged and can find a place where they are accepted just the way they are and their problems are understood.

Sexual harassment

Sexual harassment includes unwelcome sexual advances, requests for sexual favors, remarks about a person's sex, and other verbal or physical harassment of a sexual nature. The victim or abuser can be either a male or female and can be the victim's supervisor, supervisor in another area, a coworker, or non-employee (U.S. Equal

Employment Opportunity Commission n.d.c). Due to the maturity of the subject matter, the instructional materials for this portion of the workshop need to match the social-emotional level of the middle and high school students that make up the class. It's also necessary to communicate to parents in advance of when this subject matter is being covered and to get written parental approval that allows their child to participate in the discussion or lets them opt their child out of that day's class.

What is the Americans with Disabilities Act (ADA)?

The Americans with Disabilities Act (or ADA) of 1990 is a civil rights law that prohibits private employers, state and local governments, employment agencies, and labor unions from discriminating against individuals with disabilities. It contains five titles or sections, and Title 1 covers all aspects of employment including job application procedures, hiring, firing advancement, compensation, and job training. The purpose of the law is to ensure that people with disabilities have the same rights and opportunities as everyone else. It is regulated by the United States EEOC and enforced by the United States Department of Justice. In the workshop, we only cover Title 1.

What disabilities are covered under the ADA?

Under Title 1 of the ADA, an individual with a disability is someone who has a physical or mental impairment that substantially limits one or more major life activities, has a record of an impairment, or is regarded as having an impairment. This includes autism, diabetes, cancer, an intellectual impairment, mobility challenges requiring the use of a wheelchair, cerebral palsy, post-traumatic stress disorder, and multiple sclerosis (U.S. Equal Employment Opportunity Commission n.d.).

How does the ADA affect individuals in the workplace?

Under the ADA, employers are required to provide to qualified employees "reasonable accommodations" that do not impose an "undue hardship." Reasonable accommodations are defined as adjustments or modifications provided by an employer to enable a job applicant or employee with a disability equal employment opportunities in all aspects of work. This includes applying for a job, performing essential job functions, and enjoying equal access to the workplace. Undue hardship is defined as any actions requiring significant difficulty or expense on the operation of the employer's business considering the size, financial resources, and nature and structure of the operation.

The type of accommodations that an individual is entitled to varies greatly and depends upon the needs of the applicant or the employee. An employer is not required to lower quality or production standards to make an accommodation nor are they obligated to provide personal items like glasses or hearing aids. After being hired and disclosing a disability, an employer must engage in what the law calls a "flexible interactive process," a discussion between the employer and the employee on accommodations that would be more effective and practical (U.S. Equal Employment Opportunity Commission 2002).

Under the ADA, what is considered reasonable accommodations for employees with autism?

A reasonable accommodation that must be provided is dependent upon the agreement reached between an employer and an employee. The types of accommodations vary from individual to individual, and there is no comprehensive list that exists that describes every accommodation that can be provided. These accommodations must be specific to a job and the needs of the individual and cannot impose an undue hardship upon the employer (U.S. Equal Employment Opportunity Commission n.d.).

What are examples of accommodations that would be considered reasonable under the ADA?

Below are the types of accommodations that would be easy and inexpensive for an employer to implement regardless of the size of the organization or the nature of the business.

Communication supports

- allow an employee to provide written responses instead of verbal responses

- allow an employee to bring an advocate to a performance review or disciplinary meeting.

Executive functioning/time management supports

- divide large assignments into smaller tasks
- use a wall calendar to help emphasize dates
- develop a color-code system to organize files, projects, or activities
- use a job coach to teach/reinforce organization skills
- provide a list prioritizing job activities and projects
- provide written instructions for tasks
- help an employee remember the faces of coworkers by providing a directory with pictures and providing coworkers with name tags
- provide written instructions for tasks and projects
- allow additional training time for learning new tasks.

Supports from a supervisor

- provide feedback to help an employee to target areas of improvement
- prioritize an employee's list of tasks
- provide weekly or monthly meetings with the employee to discuss workplace issues
- maintain open channels of communication between an employee and a new and old supervisor to help with transitions.

Sensory supports

- allow an employee to use a hand-held squeeze ball to provide sensory input

- provide noise-cancelling headphones to reduce noise that helps the employee focus

- relocate an employee's office away from audible or visual distractions

- provide a desk lamp in place of overhead fluorescent lighting

- allow telecommuting when possible.

Stress management

- allow an employee to make telephone calls for support

- modify an employee's work schedule.

On-the-Job social skills support

- match to a workplace mentor to provide support to the employee when needed

- provide a job coach to help learn social cues

- use training videos to demonstrate appropriate social cues

- make attendance in social functions optional. (United States Department of Labor 2013)

Can an employer discriminate against an employee because of a disability?

Discrimination in any form is in violation of federal law. Under the ADA, it is illegal to discriminate against an applicant or employee in all aspects of employment including hiring, firing, wages, job assignments, promotions, layoffs, training, benefits, and any other term or condition of employment (United States Department of Labour, Office of Disability Employment Policy 2013).

What questions and actions can and can't an employer ask of an employee with a disability?

Employers are also not allowed to ask an applicant or employee the existence or severity of a disability and cannot ask a job applicant to answer medical questions. Employers may only ask the individual to take a medical exam unless it is required for all employees and the exam must be related and consistent with the employer's business needs. After being hired, an employer can only ask medical questions or require a medical exam for documentation supporting an employee's request of accommodations (U.S. Equal Employment Opportunity Commission 2017, February).

Is an applicant or employee required to disclose their disability to their employer?

No, it's entirely voluntary for an employee to disclose a disability to their employer, but to benefit from the protections of the ADA, an employee must disclose. Once the employee discloses, the employer and employee enter a discussion to determine what these accommodations will be. If there are multiple accommodation options that would equally meet the needs of the employee, the employer may choose the option that is cheaper and easier to implement (U.S. Equal Employment Opportunity Commission 2002, October).

When and to whom should an employee disclose?

Employees should disclose their disability on a "need-to-know" basis to a person of authority within the organization that can approve any reasonable accommodations. This is usually the candidate's supervisor, but if speaking to their boss is not something they feel comfortable, they are advised to disclose to an HR manager. Under no circumstances should candidates disclose their disability to a coworker prior to disclosing to their supervisor or someone in HR.

What needs to be considered in regards to a reasonable accommodation?

When disclosing a disability, it's important that the employee identifies their specific needs and the accommodations that would best meet these needs. The following questions can help in this process:

1. What limitations does the employee with ASD experience?

2. How do these limitations affect the employee's job performance?

3. What specific job tasks are a problem because of these limitations?

4. What accommodations are available to reduce or eliminate these problems?

5. Are all possible resources being used to determine accommodations?

6. Can the employee with ASD provide information on possible accommodation solutions?

7. Once accommodations are in place, would it be useful to meet with the employee with ASD to evaluate the effectiveness of the accommodations and to determine whether additional accommodations are needed?

8. Do supervisory personnel and employees need training regarding ASD?

What do you instruct candidates to do when they experience a violation of their rights?

It's important for candidates to know what their rights are as an employee so when they have a problem, they can discuss it from an informed perspective. If they experience any problems at work, they should always first speak to their immediate supervisor, but if that is not possible or it makes them uncomfortable, they should speak to HR. They should also speak to HR if they've spoken to their supervisor and the issue is not resolved to their satisfaction. If all these efforts fail, they may choose to report their grievance to the appropriate local, state, or federal government agency that is responsible for overseeing the matter.

Candidates should make all efforts to resolve their issues with their company before reporting the matter to a government agency. If these efforts fail, then this may be necessary. But, candidates need to consider the possible consequences that may arise from these actions. This will most likely upset their employer and probably their coworkers, too. Even though they are protected under the law, they may still get fired. They may be ostracized by coworkers that they thought were their friends. By considering all the long-term implications of their actions, they will be better prepared for what might happen next. We share the following contact information for the various agencies regarding a workplace grievance with the candidates: Wage and Hour Division;[1] Family and Medical Leave Act;[2] OSHA;[3] ADA.[4]

What information do you provide on the topic of conflict resolution in the workplace?

Conflict is an inevitable part of any relationship, but workplace conflicts left unresolved can create intense personal animosity and dislike among coworkers. Conversely, workplace conflicts that are effectively resolved can bring hidden problems to the surface and provide an opportunity to clear any unresolved issues so they don't erupt into larger conflicts later. Going through the process of effectively resolving conflicts helps to expand people's awareness and gives them insight into how they can achieve their goals without undermining others. Effective conflict resolution can help team members develop a stronger sense of mutual respect and a renewed faith in their ability to work together (Mindtools 2011).

---

1   www.dol.gov/wecanhelp/howtofilecomplaint.htm
2   Call 866 487 9243.
3   www.osha.gov/workers/file_complaint.html or call 800 321 6742.
4   www.ada.gov/filing_complaint.htm

What is the Thomas-Kilmann Conflict Mode Instrument for conflict resolution?

The Thomas-Kilmann Conflict Mode Instrument (TKI) is the leading measure of conflict-handling behavior. It effectively breaks down the ways to quickly assess a conflict and choose the best method to resolution to a conflict resolve it (Kilmann and Thomas 1975). For candidates, it provides an easy-to-use tool to quickly assess a workplace conflict and choose the most effective method to resolve it.

These are the five TKI conflict management strategies and the pros and cons associated with each one:

1 Accommodate

This strategy is a form of "giving in" and letting the other person in the conflict have their way.

Pros: It quickly resolves the conflict.

Cons: The person that is doing the accommodating may become resentful.

2 Avoid

This strategy postpones resolving the conflict indefinitely.

Pros: Time may help the conflict resolve itself.

Cons: The conflict and bad feelings may increase the longer the conflict is left unresolved.

3 Collaborate

This strategy requires integrating multiple ideas to help resolve a conflict.

Pros: If effectively used, a solution will be reached that is acceptable to everyone.

Cons: It takes time and may be difficult to get all parties to agree.

4 Compromise

This strategy requires all parties to give up something to find a solution that is acceptable to all parties.

Pros: Once reached, the solution will seem fair to all parties.

Cons: It takes time and may be difficult to get each person to give up something.

5 Compete

This strategy pits coworkers against one another and has a definite winner and loser in the resolution of the conflict.

Pros: It works best in an emergency or crisis when time is of the essence in finding a solution.

Cons: It pits people against one another, and the loser will probably harbor resentment.

Putting TKI into Action

Role playing is the best way to help candidates assess effective conflict resolution using all five management strategies. The final chapter contains a list of situations where candidates can learn to associate which strategies work best in a variety of settings.

What is the Interest-Based Relational Approach to conflict resolution?

The Interest-Based Relational (IBR) Approach was developed by Roger Fischer, William Ury, and Brian Patton as a negotiation strategy, but the basic premise of the IBR Approach makes it well suited for use in workplace conflicts. The IBR Approach requires users to use empathetic listening to effectively resolve conflict. If used effectively, the process can help everyone feel respected, understood, and their point of view acknowledged (Fisher, Ury, and Patton 2011).

The IBR Approach requires the all participants to do the following:

- listen with empathy and see the conflict from each other's point of view

- explain issues clearly and concisely
- encourage people to use "I" rather than "you" statements so no one feels attacked
- be clear about their feelings
- remain flexible and adaptable.

These are the steps in the IBR Approach:

Step 1. Make sure good relationships are a priority

Treat others with respect and acknowledge their viewpoint even if you don't agree. Be mindful during your discussion—stay calm, exercise acceptance, and be patient.

Step 2. Separate people from problems

Separate the issue from the person. Put personal feelings aside and address only matter that is causing the conflict.

Step 3. Listen carefully to different interests

Keep the conversation courteous and don't place blame the other person. Ask for the other person's perspective to identify the issue that the person thinks is causing the conflict.

Step 4. Listen first, talk second

Listen to other people's points of view without defending your own. Make sure that each person has finished talking before speaking. Identify what the person thinks is the issue and ask questions if you need clarification.

Step 5. Determine out the facts

Be fair and balanced in the gathering of information. Acknowledge the other person's feelings. Make sure the person feels listened to and has been a part of the discussion.

Step 6. Explore options together

By this point, the conflict may have already been resolved once everyone's views have been heard and understood, but it's important to be open to an alternate position. If needed, brainstorm ideas and be open to all suggestions to come to an agreement that will result in a satisfying outcome (Mindtools 2011).

Putting the RBI Approach into action

Role playing is the best way to help candidates practice conflict resolution. The final chapter has a list of scenarios that candidates can use to practice their conflict resolution skills using the RBI Approach.

What information does the workshop cover in regards to dating coworkers?

A decade ago, dating someone at the same company was expressly forbidden, but that is no longer the case. Since adults spend most of their week at their job, the workplace offers the best opportunity to meet people and find friends, and some of these friendships may become romantic.

To be sure that their personal life doesn't negatively affect their work life, we teach candidates the following rules:

1 Don't date your boss

Most employers have policies that prohibit employees from dating a direct supervisor or a subordinate, and this is for good reason. If the relationship sours, the disgruntled employee could claim a hostile work environment and could sue the company for harassment. A manager-subordinate romance can also create a perception of favoritism for the subordinate, which can upset the other coworkers that also report to the same manager.

2 You can only ask your coworker out one time

If a candidate wants to ask out a coworker, they only have one chance. If they continually ask a coworker out after being told no the first time, the coworker could claim a hostile working environment and report the incident to HR. The consequence of these actions at best would be a bad reputation with coworkers and at worst could result in being fired from their job.

3 Avoid public displays of affection

If a candidate is dating someone, it isn't considered professional to kiss or hug in the office. These actions can make other people uncomfortable and could possibly make some of their coworkers jealous.

4 Tell your company

It's best to disclose to a supervisor when they start dating a coworker. Disclosing a relationship to an employer will keep them from being the focus of office gossip and avoid any awkward situation at work when word finally gets out.

5 Set boundaries

Spending all your time with a boyfriend and girlfriend might not be good for their relationship. If they ever starting dating a coworker, we let them know it's okay to schedule time for being by themselves and other friends participating in the hobbies and activities that they enjoy most (Stoeffel 2015).

Part II

WORKSHOP STRUCTURE

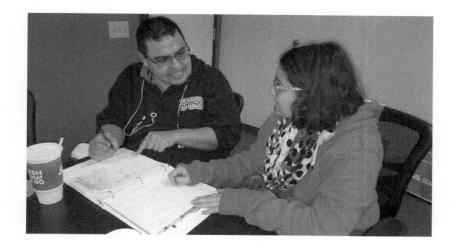

Chapter 9

Behavior, Behavior, Behavior

It's important to be mindful of our behavior so we don't disrupt the workplace.

Chris Grayson

This chapter will take the reader through the process of understanding that behavior is meaningful for the individual, has a function, and can be addressed through Positive Behavior Support (PBS).

People display behavior every second, hour, and minute of the day by breathing, walking, running, dancing, and so on. Some behavior is unacceptable – it is socially inappropriate and ultimately is not going to serve the individual. The goal is to redirect the socially unacceptable behavior and teach skills to replace the inappropriate behavior in order for the individual to be successful. PBS emphasizes respecting, valuing, dignifying, understanding, and listening to individuals that may display "behavior problems."

The four different functions of behavior for all individuals will be explored in this chapter, as well as PBS strategies. By providing appropriate learning environments including dance, classroom, and community, which are supportive and creative for the individual, we want to positively reward them for behavior that we want to see again and again over time.

What should a behavior plan look like?
Tools for challenging behaviors

One of the primary core challenges of a diagnosis of autism manifests in the area of behavior. Early behavioral intervention strategies can dramatically increase the quality of life for individuals with ASD by enhancing the possibilities of increased educational, social, and independent or supported living skills. The key to behavioral remediation lies with consistent early intervention strategies delivered at the onset of diagnosis.

Educators, therapists, and researchers agree that early intervention is the key to problem behaviors with individuals with ASD. Behavior Analysis is the science of behavior and Applied Behavior Analysis (ABA) refers to a systematic and scientific approach to the assessment and evaluation of behavior, and the applications of interventions such as PBS to alter these behaviors. ABA is a *methodology* used to teach new skills and PBS is a *strategy* used to modify behaviors that are unwanted by reinforcing appropriate behavior. Punishments such as "benching" and "time out" are not used as strategies in PBS but are found in the ABA method.

What studies indicate is that when PBS strategies are implemented early on, then the individual benefits greatly by an overall "increased quality of life." Behavior issues make it difficult to make and maintain friends and often these individuals, after leaving the school setting, find themselves in the spare back room of their family home alone, without friends, watching DVDs or at the computer day in and day out. Mainstreaming and full inclusion do not guarantee friends, as many children—even after being mainstreamed or fully included— often lack the social skills to sustain the friendships that would normally travel with them throughout their academic lives and on into their post academic living and workplaces. Negative or disruptive behaviors in the home and school setting in the early years distance our children from their peers, impeding and limiting their ability to ultimately make and keep friends, get a job, and live a life of quality.

What is Positive Behavior Support (PBS)?

According to IDEA 1997, PBS is the recommended form of intervention for dealing with challenging behavior in children with disabilities. Andrea M. Cohn of the National Association of School Psychologists defines PBS as follows:

> Positive Behavioral Support (PBS) is an empirically validated, function-based approach to eliminate challenging behaviors and replace them with prosocial skills. Use of PBS decreases the need

for more intrusive or aversive interventions (i.e., punishment or suspension) and can lead to both systemic as well as individualized change. (Cohn 2001)

First and foremost, to address a behavioral plan for the students we must know what the function of the behavior is for that specific individual in the specific environmental setting that the behavior occurs.

Determining the function of the behavior

Despite IDEA calling for PBS to be used with our students, in many cases, it is not. Often, staff have not been properly trained in implementation of the strategies, and more often than not, even those who have been trained find it difficult to put the concepts into play when they are confronted with the behavior in a real-life, everyday situation. PBS is the only IDEA behavioral intervention strategy specifically "required" for behavioral management. It has long been a component of IDEA because it is a simple, direct ideological method that works. Once the function of the behavior, or the "purpose the behavior serves" for the child has been determined, then the IEP Behavior Plan can be written.

There are several ways to determine the function of a behavior; the tool most often used is the Motivational Assessment Scale (MAS), developed by V. Mark Durand PhD and Daniel B. Crimmins, PhD (Durand and Crimmins 1992). Functional communication training is an empirically validated approach to PBS for challenging behavior (Durand and Merges 2001).

A simple and easy to use tool, the MAS is a quick way to understand the purpose underlying the problem behavior. The purpose or function for the behavior is broken down into four main categories:

1. attention-seeking

2. avoidance or escape

3. tangible/to get something

4. sensory/it feels good.

Once we determine the function of the behavior for the individual, then we go about replacing the negative or unwanted behavior by positively rewarding the desired or appropriate replacement behavior.

The intention is that over a period of time the acceptable behavior (i.e. the behavior that we are looking for) will replace the unacceptable behavior because we have positively reinforced the acceptable behavior and ignored or given 'if…then' contingencies for the negative behavior. For example, let's take hitting as a behavior that we want to shape, fade, and extinguish. We might say, "*if* you don't hit anyone in the next hour (use a timer) *then* you can use the computer for 15 minutes (use a timer).' Make sure to allow the student to have the reinforcement that he earned if he does not hit anyone within the designated hour. We have to be consistent in our delivery of the reinforcer. A good idea is to take a reinforcer inventory and make a list of the reinforcements that will help change the behavior. If a student doesn't care about puzzles then don't use puzzles as a reinforcement. The reinforcers must be meaningful for the individual.

Primary reinforcers are biological; food, drink, and pleasure are the principal examples of primary reinforcers. We can shape, fade, and extinguish behavior the quickest with primary reinforcers. Secondary reinforcers would be token economies, Legos, computers, iPads, puzzles etc.

Implementing PBS strategies: "The Big Three" components of PBS

"Catch 'em being good" is a phrase coined by PBS people who use positive reinforcement strategies to modify negative or unwanted behavior. The theory is that a reward is given for positive behavior or the behavior that is appropriate and nothing is taken away when negative behavior occurs. We strive to choose a positive reinforcement after positive behavior occurs rather than thinking in terms of punishment following negative behavior. Positive and negative reinforcement can be understood in the simplest terms as the following. A positive reinforcement is when something good happens after a behavior, whereas negative reinforcement is when something bad happens after a behavior.

For example, if you pick up trash on your school yard and put it in the trash bin then you get a ticket to be used at the school store on Friday (token reward system): something good happened after the behavior of picking up trash. On the other hand, if you run a red light and a policeman catches you then you get a ticket, your insurance fees go up and you might even have to attend driver's school. Something bad happened after a behavior or negative reinforcement occurred.

In our fast-paced modern society, we often have a difficult time positively rewarding other people in our daily life or telling others what a great job they have done or how proud we are of their accomplishments. Furthermore, the truth is that societies often have a difficult time with the "idea" of positively rewarding its individuals who have demonstrated "bad" or inappropriate behaviors, a perfect example is the American overcrowded prison system where punishment is valued over rehabilitation.

Let's take another example. A student has inappropriate behavior while getting off the bus. Whether the "behavior" happened immediately prior to school or earlier in the school day, the student may still be being punished three or four hours later for a behavior that occurred in the morning hours. The logic often used is that the child should have to endure the *punishment* for his actions for however long the school aide or teacher deems appropriate, and that the punishment matches the inappropriate "behavior." So the student is put in "time out." Let's say that time out serves no positive outcome for the individual; rather we are asking a child to sit and do "nothing" and often, we even hear, you can sit there and "think about what you've done wrong." I believe it is safe to say that no adult would adhere to this ridiculous form of time-wasting agenda and we can rest assured that the child is not sitting there in his room thinking about what he did wrong.

The thinking is this: if the student is negatively punished, benched, or put in time out for a certain period of time "equally equivalent to the inappropriate behavior," then he will certainly remember *not* to do that again! Right? Wrong! Of course, what happens most often is that the child's anger escalates while he is in "time out" and as soon as he returns to his desk or activity he usually begins to demonstrate inappropriate behavior again. And so it goes; the adult runs around behind the student continuously punishing him for his inappropriate behaviors never understanding the function of the behavior or how the behavior actually served the student while he was demonstrating it in the environment in which the behavior occurred. The taking away of stars and earned points on the board in school, benching at recess, and "time out" at school and home are all punishment strategies that results in continued inappropriate classroom and home behavioral problems because we have succeeded in only temporarily stopping the student from doing the behavior rather than working to shape, fade, and extinguish it by understanding how the behavior functions for the individual. Was it to gain attention from an adult or peer? Was it to escape or avoid something in the environment that is too difficult for the individual? Punishment generally serves to escalate an individual who is already angry and typically leaves a chain of unwanted behaviors in its aftermath. We now outline the three components of PBS.

1 State the rule

State the rule or unwanted behavior. As an example, the adult/teacher/ parent says, "The rule is no calling another student an inappropriate name." Then we ask the student to repeat the rule by asking him, "What's the rule?" The student repeats, "I shouldn't call him an inappropriate name." The student states the rule afterwards, allowing him to cognitively "map" the information in the brain. Here comes the important part: immediately after the student verbally states and repeats the rule, reward the student with, "I like the way you are thinking," and/or a high five. We want to model the behavior that we are seeking or have asked for, and then *reward* (reinforce) the behavior that the student displays.

2 "If…then" contingencies

These are "if…then" statements, best stated in the affirmative, or what we expect the student to do and what good things will happen when he follows through with what we have asked for in the "rule." In keeping with our student who has called another student an inappropriate name, you say, "*if* you do not call anyone by an inappropriate name from now until lunchtime *then* you can have 15 minutes free time on the computer in the afternoon."

We all respond to positive reinforcement; here is a simple case in point. *If* we go to work *then* we get a paycheck. When we show up for work and do our job then we get a paycheck. We are being positively rewarded for our good work with a reinforcement or paycheck. Now, if our employer says that due to the economy, we will not be getting paid, then it is highly unlikely that we will return to work the following day. By working hard and getting a paycheck we are being rewarded for our work well done. It is no different for our children.

Our student doesn't call anyone by an inappropriate name for the next three hours so he gets 15 minutes on the computer in the afternoon as promised. More importantly, when the student adheres to the if…then contingency we cannot assume that the student knows that he has displayed the behavior that we were seeking and then withhold the reward (think of the paycheck analogy). We must reward him with the reward that we promised in the if…then contingency each time immediately after he exhibited the behavior that we were asking of him until the behavior has been extinguished.

What generally falls away from the initial PBS program is the *reward* or reinforcement; then parents, teachers, and aides report that the behavior plan (PBS) is not working, when in fact, the reward is missing. We all work for rewards in our life, and without them, we become unmotivated. When we are hungry, we eat. When we go to work, we get a paycheck. *If* the student doesn't hit *then* he can have computer time.

3 Two choices

When we redirect, we want to give two choices instead of making the choice for the individual; this allows the individual to have some measure of power and control over his life. We are not empowered when we are told what to do. For example, "work on this worksheet," is not empowering, but "do you want to work on the worksheet or take a break for a few minutes?" is empowering. Always give the option of "two choices."

Reinforcement is the *key*! The "Big 3" will help us to shape, fade, and eventually extinguish unwanted behavior. The important thing to remember is that the classroom, community, and work environment shouldn't be a "battle ground." It's easy; just remember to say, "I like the way you're thinking!'

Chapter 10

Group and Candidate Requirements

Creating a safe environment

One of the most important elements directly correlated to achievement for youth with disabilities that leads to success is the ability for the teachers and administrators to create an environment where the student is free to be who they are without fear of being dismissed for their point of view or the way that they think.

Typically-developing children start forming friendships in kindergarten. By third grade, they start to coalesce into social groups based on their common interests. By the end of high school, they have learned how to form solid friendships with their peers, which become the foundation for a successful transition after high school to the next phase of their lives, which is usually college or trade school and ultimately a meaningful job in their field of interest.

This progression of social connectedness many times does not happen for individuals with autism. Due to their atypical development and challenges with social communication, many have a difficult time forming friendships or becoming part of a larger social group. Because of these differences, they can be rejected, ostracized, and bullied by their peers. These students can develop deep psychological scars from their high school experience which can make it difficult for them to successfully transition after they graduate from high school.

When putting together a group, it's important that all candidates feel accepted and welcomed so they are motivated to learn and participate in the workshop. For middle and high school students, this can be especially important, particularly if they are experiencing social isolation or mistreatment by their peers. For these students, the workshop can provide an opportunity to become part of a group of like-minded peers where they are accepted just the way they are.

By creating a safe place for students that are socially stigmatized and labeled as being different or weird, the workshop can become somewhere they are welcomed and appreciated for who they are. By providing these students with this opportunity, we are creating hope and changing lives by giving our candidates the opportunity to feel like they are in a place where they truly belong.

Setting guidelines

To help communicate the expected behaviors in the workshop, AWN created a document entitled **Workshop Expectations** [28] which explains the expected behaviors for all candidates. To help establish these guidelines, the Workshop Expectations need to be reviewed with candidates at the meeting of the first class and whenever a new member joins the group. If there are any violations in these expectations, the rules need to be revisited and clear and consistent consequences implemented each time a violation occurs. Learning how to abide by expected behaviors is not just important when interacting in a classroom. These behaviors are also essential life skills that the students will need in the workplace to keep their job and be accepted by their coworkers.

Candidate requirements

The goal of the workshop is to provide candidates with the pre-employment skill sets they will need to successfully transition into meaningful employment after graduation from high school so they can become active members of their communities. Because individuals with autism can vary widely in their skills and abilities, it's important to make sure that the program is an appropriate placement for every candidate. It is also important to consider any necessary supports or accommodations to ensure that the candidate can successfully access the program curriculum.

The following should be considered when assessing candidates for admission to workshop.

Candidates must have the ability to attend class meetings and field trips without causing a disruption.

The goal of the workshop is to prepare candidates for permanent job placements. In order to be accepted into the AWN program, candidates must have the ability attend a two-hour class or participate in a community-based activity without incident. If a candidate does not have that ability, they are not ready for a job placement and should not participate in the workshop. An individual with aggressive behavioral tendencies will disrupt the learning environment and pose a health and safety issue for anyone participating in the class. Candidates with aggressive behaviors also create a public liability while out in the community during activities like field trips and AWN-organized activities.

When considering accepting new candidates, it's essential to ask parents and caregivers about the candidate's history regarding outbursts, meltdowns, and aggressive tendencies towards others as well as any incidents of property damage. If there is a history of behavioral or emotional instability, you'll need to gather more information about the candidate including how recent these incidents were and the severity and frequency of past episodes. If this is an area of concern, ask for permission to speak to a counselor or therapist that is currently treating the candidate and ask for their opinion about placement in the workshop. For middle or high school students, you should check with the student's counselors and teachers and get their opinion about whether they feel the workshop is an appropriate placement.

Candidates must be able to independently operate a computer or operate a computer with support.

The ability to use a computer is an essential life skill, and the workshop incorporates the use of a computer as part of classroom instruction. For candidates to successfully access this element of the AWN program, they must have adequate keyboarding skills to keep up with the pace of the class, a basic understanding of how to use a computer, and knowledge of how to access the internet. For candidates that cannot use a computer independently, have no emotional or behavioral issues, and are motivated to participate, assume that an aide will be required and incorporate this support as part of the workshop for that student. Supports should be faded and eventually eliminated only after a candidate is able to independently operate a computer.

Chapter 11

Classroom Requirements

Room set-up

To help give candidates the sense that they are at a job, the environment should simulate as closely as possible a workplace conference room or break room. It's important that all candidates are facing one another. If the program is being offered in a school classroom, desks should be arranged in a circle can so candidates can see each other during classroom instruction.

Wifi

Confirm that the location where your class is being held provides wifi and that there isn't a firewall that prevents access to the internet. If wifi is not available, many smart phones can be used as a mobile wifi hotspot. Make sure the plan for the phone that you are using has enough data available so class usage doesn't exceed the minutes on the plan. Overage fees can be expensive, and switching to a plan with more minutes may be less expensive than the overage fees.

Equipment
Computers

Each student will need a computer with wifi capabilities. If you are purchasing computers for your program, Chromebook computers are a great choice due to their relatively low cost (most can be purchased for between $125 and $200) and their ease in connecting to Google and the apps that are used in class. For the instructor's computer, it must be compatible with an HDMI cable in order to connect to the projector.

Projector

During instruction using the computer, materials are projected on a blank wall so all candidates can view together the materials that are being covered. The projector must be HDMI compatible and have sound capabilities.

Screen

If the room does not have a blank wall or a pull down screen where classroom materials can be projected, you will need to purchase a portable screen.

Chapter 12

Classroom Meetings

Class structure

Each class has a specific structure that follows an order. All the classroom materials referenced in this chapter are included in the final chapter.

Part 1: Agenda and Introductions

The agenda is reviewed and any guests that are visiting the class are introduced now. The introduction lasts about five minutes.

Part 2: Roundtable Discussion

The Roundtable Discussion lasts between 40 and 45 minutes and includes the following:

Assessing a candidate's internal state of mind

Using the **AWN Incredible 5-Point Group Check in Scale** [13], candidates identify their internal state on a scale of 1 to 5. To help candidates gauge their feelings, a "1" on the scale is how they feel when they are doing what they love and a "5" is when they are angry and have lost control. Just as at work, being at a level "1" or "2" is appropriate for the situation, but at a level 3, it's time to implement proactive stress management techniques to help them bring themselves down to a level "1" or "2".

Practicing stress management techniques

After the group check in, the class does a group stretch for three to four minutes. Usually during the first meeting of the month, the group practices a **Mindful Breathing Exercise** [16]. You can also incorporate your own mindful exercises that you create yourself or search for audio clips or videos on Google or YouTube that you can play in class.

Learning about appropriate workplace topics

Using icebreakers, candidates are able to share information about themselves so other members of the group can learn something about them (see the list of **Icebreaker Questions** in the Instructor Materials section and the **Icebreaker Worksheet** [12]). These questions are also appropriate topics for workplace conversations, and the exercise helps candidates learn about the types of questions that are appropriate to ask coworkers to get to know them better.

Practicing workplace conversational skills

This exercise helps candidates learn how to share information about what they did during the week and any upcoming plans they may have. This is similar to workplace discussions that happen on Friday when coworkers ask about your upcoming weekend plans and on Monday when coworkers ask what you did over the weekend. Using the **Your Week Worksheet—What Happened with You?** [11], candidates summarize the who, what, where, when, and favorite part of these activities and use this as a guide to create the narrative of their week. To make the activity more interactive, candidates are paired and using the **Your Week Worksheet—Interview your Partner** [11], they interview their partner about what happened in their week. After they finish their interviews, candidates share with the group what they learned about their partner.

Inspirational quote

About once a month, an inspirational quote is introduced with a discussion of how it applies to work. There is an endless number of questions that are appropriate to use in this part of the Roundtable Discussion, and a list is included in the last chapter.

Guest speakers

Any speakers are scheduled in the Roundtable Discussion.

Part 3: Prepare and Practice

This portion of the workshop is used to prepare candidates for upcoming events and to send thank you emails to field trip hosts. A workplace topic is introduced and discussed during this time. Prepare and Practice lasts between 35 and 40 minutes and includes the following:

Preparation for upcoming events

This part of the workshop is to prep candidates about upcoming field trips and AWN events. This includes:

- viewing the website of the organization for next field trip

- assigning candidate questions for the next field trip (these are prepared in advance by the instructors)

- using the **Time Management Worksheet** [18] and Google maps to estimate time candidate's travel for the next field trip

- deciding upon the method of transportation for each candidate and arranging carpools for candidates that live close to one another

- deciding on the type of attire that matches company culture for a future field trip.

Field trip follow-up

At the next class meeting after the field trip, a thank you email is sent to the field trip host. The instructor's email account is projected so candidates can view the email as it is being composed. This exercise helps candidates learn how to write a thank you email after an interview.

Monthly topics

This portion of the workshop is used to focus on a specific work-related topic. A new topic is covered each month, except for Interview Essentials, which is covered over two months:

Months 1 and 2: Getting organized with Google, assessments, workplace paperwork and time management, syncing candidate smart phones

The first two months of the workshop are used to give candidates a foundational knowledge of the apps on Google, identify career and workplace preferences, and become familiar with the paperwork used when applying for a job.

Getting organized with Google

By the end of the first meeting, candidates have a Gmail account or have confirmed that they have a Gmail account with a work-appropriate user name. By the end of the second month, candidates have:

- created their resume and list of references on Google Docs

- learned about Gmail formatting options

- used Calendar to input workshop dates for the next month—this continues throughout the workshop as events and activities are scheduled

- used Tasks to document homework assignments and due dates—this continues throughout the workshop as assignments are assigned.

Assessments

All assessments should be completed during the first month of the workshop. After the **Interests Inventory** [36] and **Work Smarts assessment** [38] are completed, the results are tabulated on a Google sheet (a program similar to Excel) and the sheet is projected and shared with all candidates so they can see who has similar interests and learning styles. Instructors should scan each assessment, save in their Google Drive, and share in Drive with candidates a copy of their completed assessment.

Workplace paperwork

By the end of the second month, all candidates should have completed the **Employment Application** [7], a **Form W-4** [8], and a **Form I-9** [9]. Candidates should also scan and save on Drive a copy of their social security card and ID (driver's license, state ID card or passport). Middle or high school students that do not have a license or state ID may use their school ID.

Time Management Worksheet

By the end of the meeting of the second class, candidates are instructed in the use of the **Time Management Worksheet** [18] to determine time travel from their home to the class. It is also used for each upcoming field trip to help candidates determine what time they need to leave their house to be on time for the meeting.

Syncing candidate smartphones

By the end of the second month, candidates that have a smartphone should have the Google apps covered in class synced to their phone.

Month 3: Dress for success

By this time, candidates have already gone on one or two field trips, so they have been introduced to matching attire to the culture of the workplace. To reinforce this concept, the presentation, **Can I Wear This to Work?** is shown to the class. Candidate's measurements are also taken and recorded on the **Measurement Worksheet** [20] so they know their correct sizes for various articles of clothing when they go shopping, both online and at a retail store. This topic only requires two to three meetings to cover since the field trips provide ongoing instruction on this topic.

Month 4: Interview essentials

Due to the amount of information covered, this topic takes two months to cover all the information. This includes:

Interview Prep Checklist and Interview Reflection Checklist

These worksheets cover everything a candidate needs to do before, during, and after an interview; how to reflect on an interview performance; and how to improve their performance in their next interview. The information on these worksheets is reviewed in class.

Candidates are instructed to use these worksheets every time they go on an interview.

Mock interviews

Using the **AWN Ambassador Job Description** [21]as a reference, candidates participate in a mock interview in front of the class. After the interview is completed, the group is quizzed on what the candidate did well and areas for improvement. These interviews should be videotaped and, if possible, privately reviewed with the candidate to help them view their facial expressions and body language.

10 Frequently Asked Interview Questions

These questions are reviewed and at least two are used during the mock interview. Candidates are instructed to use practice the answers for an upcoming interview.

Elevator Pitch Essentials

This information reviews how candidates can personalize their own elevator pitch for use during interviews, networking events, and when introducing themselves. Using the **Elevator Pitch Worksheet** [21] candidates create their own elevator pitch and then rehearse it in front of the group for constructive feedback.

Month 5: Connecting to coworkers (CTC)

The focus of instruction in CTC is making a good first impression, and using stress management to maintain a positive relationship with coworkers and supervisors. Conflict resolution techniques are introduced and covered more in depth during Understanding the Workplace.

Month 6: Networking and landing a job

The essentials of scheduling and conducting an informational interview are covered in this section. Candidates have been practicing their informational interview skills during the monthly field trips, so they have already been introduced to the process. Candidates also learn the elements of networking and how to use social media as part of their job search.

Month 7: Understanding the workplace

Candidates learn about the structure of an organization and about the roles that a variety of jobs play within that structure. Candidates also learn about important labor laws and review the Americans with Disabilities Act and how it is relevant in the workplace. Conflict resolution techniques are reviewed and role-playing activities are used to help candidates put these techniques into practice.

Month 8: Workshop review

This month is used to review all the information that was covered in the workshop. For candidates that did not start the program from the beginning, this is an opportunity to review any information that was missed.

Part 4: Recall and Review

This part of the workshop is used to review the information that was covered in class and recall information they learned about another candidate. Candidates take a 5-questions quiz as a group; the quiz contains four multiple choices questions and one true and false. One question is about a member of the group, and, if an upcoming event was discussed in class, at least one question is related to the event. Recall and Review lasts about 10 minutes.

Chapter 13

Field Trips

Field trips are scheduled once per month and provide candidates with an opportunity to put into practice the skills they have learned in class. This includes estimating time travel, choosing attire that matches the company culture, researching an organization, and preparing questions for an interview.

If time allows, arrange for the group to meet for dinner after lunch, or before the meeting. This provides a fun shared experience for the group and an opportunity for candidates to practice their conversational skills over a meal. It also allows instructors an opportunity to observe how well candidates are generalizing their conversational skills in a different environment than the classroom. Parents and caregivers are not allowed to accompany their son or daughter on the field trip, but they may be invited to social events like a dinner after a field trip. This also becomes a time for parents and caregivers to socialize with each other, candidates, and program instructors.

Choosing a business

Almost any business is suitable for a field trip visit. The most motivating places for candidates will be with a company that hires in their preferred field of interest. The easiest to schedule are places where you have a direct contact. It is possible to successfully schedule a field trip with an organization where you don't have a contact, but you'll need to practice the elevator pitch about your program so you can quickly decide what you want and the mission of your organization. Review the website of the company you want to visit prior to making your call so you are familiar with what the company does, the goods and services it provides, and the names of the senior managers of the company.

Scheduling a field trip

Once you have identified a business you would like to visit, do a Google search for the organization's address and phone number. A phone call is the best way to make your initial contact, so make sure you sound professional and have no interruptions during your call. If the organization is large and you do not have a name of anyone that is employed within the organization, ask to be connected to the human resources department. If the company or store is small in size ask for the owner or the manager.

Below is a sample telephone introduction that you can use when making your initial call.

SAMPLE TELEPHONE INTRODUCTION SCRIPT

Hello Ms. Jones. My name is Susan Osborne, and I am calling from Autism Works Now. Our organization teaches middle and high school students with autism the skills they need to get and keep a job. The current statistics for this population after they leave high school is not good with over 80 percent never holding a job or attending college within eight years of leaving high school. Our program is attempting to help these students so they have the skills to transition to meaningful employment after high school.

An important part of our program is a monthly field trip to a business, and I was hoping we could schedule a visit with your company. These visits are an important part of our program because they provide our candidates an opportunity to practice the skills they've learned in class in an authentic workplace setting and provides them with an opportunity to learn about the hiring perspectives of business owners and human resources managers. I was hoping you might be willing to host a field trip for our group on a day and time that is most convenient for you.

If your contact says yes to arranging a visit, schedule the date and time during the call. If possible, try to schedule the visit on the same day and time as the workshop; however, as you want the visit to have as low an impact as possible on the person's schedule, be flexible on the date and time. If you are not speaking to the owner of the business, president of the company, or the head of a division within the company, your contact will probably have to check with their supervisor for approval to schedule the visit. Confirm the date that your contact will have an answer, and be sure to call back on this date. Sometimes your contact will request additional information so be sure to send the email right away and no more than 24 hours after your conversation.

Follow-up emails

After your call, send a follow-up email to confirm the date and time you scheduled your field trip or an email recapping your conversation and the date you will be calling back.

SAMPLE EMAIL SCRIPT: FIELD TRIP CONFIRMATION

Dear Ms. Jones,

Thank you for your time on the phone today and thank you for hosting our next field trip with the candidates of Autism Works Now for May 5 at 2:00pm.

Our visits typically last around two hours and include a tour of the facility. Our candidates also prepare questions to ask during the visit, and if you'd like, we are happy to send a list of these in advance. Our group will include two adults and between five and eight candidates who range between 14 and 18 years old.

Thank you again for hosting our visit to the Pacific Coast Theatre in Springfield. Please let me know if you need any additional information, and I look forward to meeting you on May 5.

Sincerely,

Susan Osborne
Autism Works Now

SAMPLE EMAIL SCRIPT: FOLLOW-UP CALL BACK

Dear Ms. Jones,

Thank you for your time on the phone the other day. I've attached a copy of a brochure for Autism Works Now, and if you'd like to learn more about our organization, please visit our website at www.autismworksnow.org.

Thanks so much for considering a visit from the candidates from Autism Works Now to the Pacific Coast Theatre in Springfield, CA. Our Workplace Readiness Workshop teaches adults with autism the skills they need to get and keep jobs. Field trip visits are an important part of our program as these provide useful opportunities for our candidates to put into practice the skills that they've learned in the classroom as well as learn about the hiring perspectives of business managers and employers.

Visits typically last around two hours and include a tour of the facility. Our candidates also prepare questions to ask during the visit, and if you'd like, we are happy to send a list of these questions in advance. Our group will include two adults and between five and eight candidates who range between 14 and 18 years old. Our past visits have included meetings with the owner of Donner Ranch, the general manager of KTTT Channel 2, and the Executive Director of Home Bodies, a nonprofit that helps the elderly.

Thank you again for any help in arranging a visit for Autism Works Now to the Pacific Coast Theatre in Springfield. I will be calling next Wednesday to follow up. Please let me know if you need any additional information, and I look forward to confirming our visit.

Sincerely,

Susan Osborne
Autism Works Now

Field trip preparation
Create and share a calendar event

At the next class meeting, create a Google Calendar event and share with candidates. Also, share the event with the person that is transporting the candidate. The event will include the date, time, and address where the field trip is taking place. If candidates live close to one another, arrange for those candidates to carpool. Do not share the event with anyone that does not have a Gmail account. There is an incompatibility issue with Google and non-Gmail accounts. These recipients will receive a notification of the event but it will contain an incorrect date and time.

Estimate time travel

Help each candidate determine travel time to the business address using Google Maps. If needed, use the **Time Management Worksheet** [18] to help candidates decide what time they need to leave so they aren't late for the field trip. All candidates should be at the location at least 15 minutes prior to the start time of the field trip.

Review the company website

Project the website on a blank wall and review it together with the class. Be sure to go over the company's mission, the products and services they provide, and the senior managers of the company. Assign a homework assignment for candidates to review the website several times before the next class or before the field trip if the meeting is happening before the next class.

Matching attire to the company's culture

Discuss the type of business that is being visited and decide what type of attire would be appropriate. If you would like to share a visual reference of type of attire that candidates can wear on the field trip, do a Google search for a companies in similar industries and share that with the class during your field trip preparation.

Assign questions

Prior to class, create enough questions to assign one per candidate. To help create your questions, review the company's website and research the company's senior managers and the person that helped arrange your field trip. A list of sample questions is included in the final chapter under Instructional Materials.

Confirm the field trip information by email

In addition to the shared Calendar event, send an email confirmation with the date, time, address, and parking instructions at least a week prior to when the field trip is happening. If the driver is the candidate's parent, they will not be accompanying their son or daughter during the field trip, so ask your host if there is a nearby café and coffee shop where they can wait while the field trip is happening. Also, include the list of questions and the name of the candidate that is assigned to each question.

Decide if the group wants to meet for dinner

Get an estimate of the number of people that will be attending and locate a restaurant in the neighborhood close to the organization you are visiting.

Confirm dinner reservations

If the group is going to dinner after the field trip, provide the address of the restaurant and the time of the reservation in your confirmation email.

SAMPLE EMAIL SCRIPT: CANDIDATE AND DRIVER EMAIL

Hi everyone,

Here is the information for our field trip and dinner on Thursday, April 21.

Field trip to Pacific Coast Theatre

Location: 123 River Street, Springfield, CA 91001

Time: 2:00pm

Early dinner at John's Grill

Location: 345 River Street (across the street from Pacific Coast)

Time: 4:30

Parking

Free parking is available in the garage next to the theatre.

Candidates, these are your questions. We will also have a print out of your question at the theatre.

Cathy: What is your favorite movie?

Clark: What are the various jobs at Pacific Coast Theatre?

Lucy: What is your favorite thing about working at Pacific Coast Theatre?

Parker: What career advice do you have for someone wanting to work at Pacific Coast Theatre?

Steven: How did you get started at the Pacific Coast Theatre?

Wyatt: What is a typical day like at Pacific Coast Theatre?

Thank you and we look forward to seeing everyone on Wednesday!

Sincerely,

Susan and Joanne

During the field trip

Instructors should meet all candidates prior to meeting with your field trip host so you can enter as a group. Let the receptionist or a company associate know that you have arrived and the name of the person you are scheduled to meet. Greet the field trip host and introduce the host to each of the candidates. Each candidate should shake the hand of the host, smile, and say hello. At the end of the field trip, thank the host for their time and let them know how much you appreciated meeting with the group. Ask for the card of the field trip host before you leave.

Take notes

Instructors should take notes during the question and answer portion of the field trip. The notes are transcribed afterwards onto a Google doc and include each candidate's question and the host's answers. These become a good resource of the types of questions that candidates can ask when they have an actual job interview.

Pictures

Take as many pictures as you can during the field trip. Be sure to take a picture at the end of the meeting with all candidates and the field trip host.

Follow-up
Thank you note

Instructors should email the host after the field trip, preferably the same day, thanking the host for their time and expressing how much the candidates learned during the visit. Attach a picture taken during the field trip, preferably one taken with the host and all candidates. In the next class at the start of Prepare and Practice, project the instructor's Gmail account and compose a group email thanking the host. Get input from the group for suggestions for the email and include each candidate's Gmail name in the cc of the email.

SAMPLE THANK YOU EMAIL SCRIPT: FROM INSTRUCTORS

Dear Mary,

We can't thank you enough for making everyone from Autism Works Now feel so welcome during our visit to Pacific Coast Theatre. The tour was so much fun, especially the projection room, and you were so generous in answering our candidates' questions. You made a very positive impact and the information you provided will serve them well in their job search.

Thanks again. You made our visit so memorable! We hope to see you next time we visit the Pacific Coast Theatre!

Sincerely,

Joanne Lara and Susan Osborne
Autism Works Now

SAMPLE THANK YOU EMAIL SCRIPT: FROM THE GROUP

Dear Mary,

Thank you so much for hosting our field trip at the Pacific Coast Theatre on Wednesday. We are all avid movie goers, and it was very informative to get a behind-the-scenes look at the projection room and the employee's break room.

We really liked the talk session at the end of our visit. We look forward to possibly one day being hired as an associate with the Pacific Coast Theatre!

Sincerely,

Cathy Anderson
Clark Davis
Lucy Johnson
Parker Smith
Steven Thompson
Wyatt Wilson

Joanne Lara, Executive Director
Susan Osborne, Workplace Readiness Director

Chapter 14

Instructional Materials

Organizing candidate binders

At the start of the program, all candidates receive their own binder. Each binder is divided into eight sections where classroom materials are filed. At the beginning of each class, materials are distributed, and candidates are responsible for placing all materials in the correct section of their binder. Support is provided for candidates that need it.

Binder materials

- 1½" binder: white (preferred color) with pocket on front

- binder dividers: 8 tab

- permanent tabs

- lined paper

- colored paper (any color): preferable to have a variety of colors that correspond to the color of each binder tab.

All materials except the permanent tabs can be purchased at almost any discount and office supply stores. The permanent tabs are available from a number of online retailers, but the least costly option is online from Office Depot: Redi-Tag® Permanent Index Tabs, Blank, White, Pack of 104 Tabs, Item # 753475. For the binder tabs, we like to use Office Depot® Brand Dividers Write-On Tabs, Assorted Colors, 8-Tab, Item #933226. Being able to directly write on the tab saves time when assembling the binders.

Binder assembly

- Each binder divider represents a segment of the workshop. Under each divider section, instructional materials are filed and numbered for easy identification.

- For each of the numbered sections, the first page is a blank sheet. The permanent tabs are numbered and attached to the right side of each sheet so they stagger down the page and don't overlap with the next divider tab.

- A table of contents for the entire binder is on the first page of the binder. A table of contents for each divider section is on the first page for that section.

- Create a personalized cover page for the binder that includes the candidate's name. If your program has a logo or trademark, also include that on the binder cover.

- At the end of each binder, 20 to 25 pieces of blank lined paper are included so candidates have a place to take notes. Use cardstock or a piece of paper in a contrasting color as the cover page for the section containing the lined paper.

Binder divider labels and numbers for instructional materials

Each binder contains a total of eight dividers and 29 numbered tabs. The following are the labels for each divider (these are bulleted) and the numbers that correspond to the instructional materials in each section.

- AGENDAS

- ASSESSMENTS

  1. Assessment Checklist

  2. General Work Knowledge Assessment

  3. Google Knowledge Assessment

  4. Interests Inventory

  5. Preferred Workplace Profile

  6. Work Smarts Assessment

- WORKPLACE PAPERWORK

  7. Employment Application

  8. Form W-4

  9. Form I-9

  10. Resume Worksheet Example

- ROUNDTABLE DISCUSSION

  11. Your Week Worksheet

    – What Happened with You?

    – Interview Your Partner

  12. AWN Icebreaker Worksheet

  13. AWN Incredible 5-Point Group Check in Scale

  14. AWN Incredible 5-Point Stress Meter

  15. AWN SODA Chart (Stop, Observe, Deliberate, Act)

  16. AWN Mindful Breathing Exercise

  17. AWN Stress Management Worksheet

- PREPARE and PRACTICE

  18. Time Management Worksheet

  19. Getting Organized with Google

    – Gmail Formatting Options

    – Google Contact Spreadsheet

  20. Dress for Success

    – Men's Measurement Worksheet

    – Women's Measurement Worksheet

  21. Interview Essentials

    – Interview Checklist

    – 10 Frequently Asked Interview Questions

- Elevator Pitch Overview
- Elevator Pitch Worksheet
- Interview Reflection Checklist
- AWN Ambassador Job Description

22. Connecting and Coworkers

- Making A Good First Impression When Starting a New Job

23. Networking and Landing a Job

- Informational Interview Essentials
- Informational Interview Contact List
- Informational Interview Scripts and Correspondence
- Informational Interview Worksheet
- Networking Worksheet
- Social Media Overview

24. Understanding the Workplace

- Workplace Hierarchy Chart
- Labor Law Overview
- Americans with Disabilities Act (ADA) Overview
- Conflict Resolution Role Playing Techniques
- AWN Rules for Dating Coworkers

• REVIEW and RECALL

25. Workshop Summary

26. Workshop Quiz

• EXPECTATIONS

27. Workplace Habits and Expectations

28. Workshop Syllabus

29. Workshop Expectations

- FIELD TRIPS and GUEST SPEAKERS

  30. Field Trip Recap—Sample

Worksheets and study guides

The following are all of the instructional materials that are used during workshop classroom instruction. They can be downloaded at www.jkp.com/catalogue/book/9781785927256.

1 ASSESSMENT CHECKLIST

Name: _____

1. General Work Knowledge
2. Google Knowledge
3. Interests Assessment
4. Preferred Workplace Profile
5. Work Smarts

2 GENERAL WORK KNOWLEDGE ASSESSMENT

Name: _____

Date: _____

Check all items that you know how to do on your own without support:

- ☐ I know how to use a computer or laptop.
- ☐ I have a smartphone.
- ☐ I know how to use a smartphone.
- ☐ I have an email address.
- ☐ I check my email at least once a day.
- ☐ I use a calendar to keep track of my appointments.
- ☐ I am familiar with Google.
- ☐ I know how to do internet research.
- ☐ II know to find an address using the internet.
- ☐ I have a Gmail address.
- ☐ I am familiar with these Google apps:
    - ☐ Drive
    - ☐ Calendar
    - ☐ Maps
    - ☐ Contacts
    - ☐ Tasks
- ☐ I know how to use the program word to type documents.
- ☐ I know how to use the program excel to draft spreadsheets.
- ☐ I know how to arrive to an appointment on time.
- ☐ An interview should take how long?
    - ☐ 15 minutes
    - ☐ 1 hour
    - ☐ 2 hours

- ☐ I have a resume.
- ☐ I have applied for a job.
- ☐ I have worked as a volunteer or held a paying job.
- ☐ I know the type of job that I want and/or have a career goal.
- ☐ I have at least 3 adult personal references.
- ☐ I have at least 3 work references.
- ☐ I know that I should bring my resume to an interview.
- ☐ I know that I should get 8 hours sleep the night before an interview.
- ☐ I know how to prepare a healthy breakfast.

★

AUTISM WORKS NOW Assessments

3 GOOGLE KNOWLEDGE ASSESSMENT

Name: _____

Date: _____

Check all items that you can do on your own without support:

- ☐ Google
    - ☐ Create a new account
    - ☐ Change my personal information
    - ☐ Change my password
- ☐ Gmail
    - ☐ Compose and send an email
    - ☐ Format an email (i.e. change text, indent, add bullets)
    - ☐ Search for an email
    - ☐ Create and edit a label
    - ☐ Set filters
    - ☐ Manage settings
        - ☐ Add a picture
        - ☐ Create a signature
        - ☐ Create a vacation responder
        - ☐ Create a folder
        - ☐ Create a filter
        - ☐ Forward emails
        - ☐ Set a theme
        - ☐ Set the "undo" send feature
- ☐ Calendar
    - ☐ Create an event with a time, date and location
    - ☐ Share an event

- ☐ Add repeat to an event
- ☐ Add location
- ☐ Add description
- ☐ Add notifications
- ☐ Change event time zone
- ☐ Change event color
- ☐ Create a calendar
- ☐ Share a calendar
- ☐ Drive
  - ☐ Create a document on Docs (like Word)
  - ☐ Create a spreadsheet on Sheets (like Excel)
  - ☐ Create a presentation on Slides (like PowerPoint)
  - ☐ Create a survey on Forms
  - ☐ Search for a document, spreadsheet, or presentation
  - ☐ Share a Doc/Sheet/Slide/Survey
  - ☐ Create a Folder
  - ☐ Move a Doc/Sheet/Slide/Survey to a folder
- ☐ Maps
  - ☐ Find an address
  - ☐ Estimate time travel
  - ☐ Check traffic
- ☐ Tasks
  - ☐ Know how to access on Gmail
  - ☐ Know how to access on Calendar
  - ☐ Add/delete a task
  - ☐ Add a task due date
- ☐ Contacts
  - ☐ Create a new contact
  - ☐ Edit a contact
  - ☐ Create a contact group

★

AUTISM WORKS NOW Assessments

4 INTERESTS INVENTORY

Name: _____

Date: _____

When you have free time and no one is telling you what to do, what do you like to do?

    1.

    2.

    3.

What do you like to talk about, read about, or do for a long period of time?

    1.

    2.

    3.

What was/is your favorite subject in school?

    1.

    2.

    3.

If you are at a bookstore or magazine stand, what type of book or magazine would you pick up?

    1.

    2.

    3.

What are your favorite sports, hobbies, or recreational activities?

    1.

    2.

    3.

What are your favorite internet sites and subject matter on those sites?

    1.

    2.

    3.

AUTISM WORKS NOW Assessments

5 PREFERRED WORKPLACE PROFILE

Name: _____

Date: _____

1. What jobs and careers are you most interested in? *List up to 10.*

_____

_____

_____

_____

_____

_____

_____

_____

_____

_____

2. List the job-specific skills, degrees, or certificates that you've received, computer programs that you are proficient in, and foreign languages that you are conversant in.

Skills:

_____

_____

Degrees or certificates:

_____

_____

Computer software programs:

_____

_____

Foreign languages

_____

_____

YOUR JOB-RELATED TALENTS AND SKILLS

Circle the words that are most applicable to you:

Acting	Advising	Analyzing *(ideas, situations)*
Assembling	Budgeting	Building
Calculating	Caring for Animals	Caring for People
Caring for Things *(plants, artwork)*	Categorizing	Classifying
Compiling	Composing Music	Coordinating *(events, work)*
Counseling	Creating	Decorating
Deciding	Demonstrating	Designing
Drawing	Editing	Estimating
Evaluating (a performance)	Examining (info, patient)	Explaining
Handling Complaints	Influencing	Initiating
Innovating	Inspecting	Interpreting *(data, languages)*
Inventing	Investigating	Leading
Listening	Meeting Deadlines	Meeting the Public
Monitoring	Motivating	Negotiating
Observing	Operating *(equipment)*	Organizing
Persuading	Photographing	Presenting
Proofreading	Public Speaking	Reasoning
Recording Information	Repairing	Researching
Scheduling	Selling	Summarizing
Supervising	Teaching	Testing
Troubleshooting	Updating	Visualizing
Writing		

★

Additional Skills:

_____

_____

_____

IMPORTANT CRITERIA AND IDEAL WORK ENVIRONMENT

How many hours do you want to work per week?

☐ Less than 10 hours

☐ Between 10 and 20 hours

☐ Between 20 and 40 hours

☐ 40 hours or more

What is your maximum commute (time and distance)?

☐ Time: _____ minutes / hours *(circle one)*

☐ Distance: _____ miles

How will you get to and from work?

☐ Drive my own car

☐ Use public transportation

☐ Walk

How much money do you need to make? *(choose at least one)*

☐ $_____ per hour

☐ $_____ per week

☐ $_____ per month

☐ $_____ per year

How much money do you want to make? *(choose at least one)*

☐ $_____ per hour

☐ $_____ per week

☐ $_____ per month

☐ $_____ per year

Are you willing/able to obtain further training or education in order to qualify for a particular job?

☐ Yes

☐ No

Do you prefer to perform the same duties every day, different duties every day, or a combination of both?

☐ Same duties every day

☐ Different duties every day

☐ Combination of both

Do you need a job that is very structured, where you know exactly what you need to do, or one that allows you to decide what tasks to do and when?

☐ Structured environment where you know what to do

☐ Allows you to decide what tasks to do and when

Do you prefer a job with a slow and steady pace or one that is fast paced?

☐ Slow and steady pace

☐ Fast paced

Can you manage a job with tight deadlines and surprise projects?

☐ Yes

☐ No

How do you prefer to work?

☐ Alone for most of the day

☐ Minimal interaction with coworkers

☐ Lots of interaction with coworkers

☐ Interaction with people inside and outside of the organization

What kind of supervision do you need?

☐ Close, including contact with my supervisor several times per day

☐ Daily check-ins

☐ Weekly supervision

☐ Prefer to be self-employed

Do you want to work indoors or outdoors?

☐ Indoors

☐ Outdoors

Do you prefer an environment that is formal or informal?

☐ Formal

☐ Informal

Do you prefer detailed, well-defined or creative/strategic work?

☐ Detailed and well-defined

☐ Creative/strategic work

Which of the following do you prefer working with?

☐ Animals

☐ Facts and information

☐ Ideas

☐ Numbers _____

_____

☐ People

☐ Your hands

What other criteria are important to you?

_____

_____

Adapted by AWN from *The Complete Guide to Getting a Job for People with Asperger's Syndrome* by Barbara Bissonnette (2013)

★

AUTISM WORKS NOW Assessments

6 WORK SMARTS SPREADSHEET

After the Work Smarts Assessment is completed, it is 3-hole punched and filed in this section of the binder.

★

AUTISM WORKS NOW Workplace Paperwork

7 EMPLOYMENT APPLICATION

Employment Application

Applicant Information

Full Name: _____ Date: _____
　　　　　　　Last　　　　　　　　*First*　　　　　　　*M.I.*

Address: _____
　　　　　Street Address　　　　　　　　　　　　　　　　*Apartment/Unit #*

_____
　　　City　　　　　　　　　　　　　　*State*　　　*ZIP Code*

Phone: _____ Email_____

Date Available: _____ Social Security No.:_____ Desired Salary:$_____

Position Applied for: _____

　　　　　　　　　　　　　　　　　　　　YES　NO
Are you a citizen of the United States?　□　□　If no, are you authorized to work in the U.S.?　YES □　NO □

　　　　　　　　　　　　　　　　　YES　NO
Have you ever worked for this company?　□　□　If yes, when?_____

　　　　　　　　　　　　　　　　　　YES　NO
Have you ever been convicted of a felony?　□　□

If yes, explain: _____

Education

High School: _____ Address:_____

　　　　　　　　　　　　　　　　　YES　NO
From: _____ To:_____ Did you graduate?　□　□　Diploma::_____

College: _____ Address:_____

　　　　　　　　　　　　　　　　　YES　NO
From: _____ To:_____ Did you graduate?　□　□　Degree:_____

Other: _____ Address:_____

　　　　　　　　　　　　　　　　　YES　NO
From: _____ To:_____ Did you graduate?　□　□　Degree:_____

References

Please list three professional references.

1

Full Name: _____ Relationship: _____

Company: _____ Phone: _____

Address: _____

Full Name: _____ Relationship: _____

Company: _____ Phone: _____

Address: _____

Full Name: _____ Relationship: _____

Company: _____ Phone: _____

Address: _____

Previous Employment

Company: _____ Phone: _____

Address: _____ Supervisor: _____

Job Title: _____ Starting Salary:$_____ Ending Salary:$_____

Responsibilities: _____

From: _____ To:_____ Reason for Leaving:_____

May we contact your previous supervisor for a reference?   YES ☐   NO ☐

_____

Company: _____ Phone: _____

Address: _____ Supervisor: _____

Job Title: _____ Starting Salary:$_____ Ending Salary:$_____

Responsibilities: _____

From: _____ To:_____ Reason for Leaving:_____

May we contact your previous supervisor for a reference?   YES ☐   NO ☐

_____

Company: _____ Phone: _____

Address: _____ Supervisor: _____

Job Title: _____ Starting Salary:$_____ Ending Salary:$_____

Responsibilities: _____

From: _____ To:_____ Reason for Leaving:_____

2

May we contact your previous supervisor for a reference?   YES ☐   NO ☐

Military Service

Branch: _____   From:_____   To:_____

Rank at Discharge: _____   Type of Discharge:_____

If other than honorable, explain: _____

Disclaimer and Signature

I certify that my answers are true and complete to the best of my knowledge.

If this application leads to employment, I understand that false or misleading information in my application or interview may result in my release.

Signature: _____   Date:_____

AUTISM WORKS NOW Workplace Paperwork

8 FORM W-4

Form W-4 (2017)

Purpose. Complete Form W-4 so that your employer can withhold the correct federal income tax from your pay. Consider completing a new Form W-4 each year and when your personal or financial situation changes.

Exemption from withholding. If you are exempt, complete **only** lines 1, 2, 3, 4, and 7 and sign the form to validate it. Your exemption for 2017 expires February 15, 2018. See Pub. 505, Tax Withholding and Estimated Tax.

Note: If another person can claim you as a dependent on his or her tax return, you can't claim exemption from withholding if your total income exceeds $1,050 and includes more than $350 of unearned income (for example, interest and dividends).

Exceptions. An employee may be able to claim exemption from withholding even if the employee is a dependent, if the employee:

• Is age 65 or older,

• Is blind, or

• Will claim adjustments to income; tax credits; or itemized deductions, on his or her tax return.

The exceptions don't apply to supplemental wages greater than $1,000,000.

Basic instructions. If you aren't exempt, complete the **Personal Allowances Worksheet** below. The worksheets on page 2 further adjust your withholding allowances based on itemized deductions, certain credits, adjustments to income, or two-earners/multiple jobs situations.

Complete all worksheets that apply. However, you may claim fewer (or zero) allowances. For regular wages, withholding must be based on allowances you claimed and may not be a flat amount or percentage of wages.

Head of household. Generally, you can claim head of household filing status on your tax return only if you are unmarried and pay more than 50% of the costs of keeping up a home for yourself and your dependent(s) or other qualifying individuals. See Pub. 501, Exemptions, Standard Deduction, and Filing Information, for information.

Tax credits. You can take projected tax credits into account in figuring your allowable number of withholding allowances. Credits for child or dependent care expenses and the child tax credit may be claimed using the **Personal Allowances Worksheet** below. See Pub. 505 for information on converting your other credits into withholding allowances.

Nonwage income. If you have a large amount of nonwage income, such as interest or dividends, consider making estimated tax payments using Form 1040-ES, Estimated Tax for Individuals. Otherwise, you may owe additional tax. If you have pension or annuity income, see Pub. 505 to find out if you should adjust your withholding on Form W-4 or W-4P.

Two earners or multiple jobs. If you have a working spouse or more than one job, figure the total number of allowances you are entitled to claim on all jobs using worksheets from only one Form W-4. Your withholding usually will be most accurate when all allowances are claimed on the Form W-4 for the highest paying job and zero allowances are claimed on the others. See Pub. 505 for details.

Nonresident alien. If you are a nonresident alien, see Notice 1392, Supplemental Form W-4 Instructions for Nonresident Aliens, before completing this form.

Check your withholding. After your Form W-4 takes effect, use Pub. 505 to see how the amount you are having withheld compares to your projected total tax for 2017. See Pub. 505, especially if your earnings exceed $130,000 (Single) or $180,000 (Married).

Future developments. Information about any future developments affecting Form W-4 (such as legislation enacted after we release it) will be posted at www.irs.gov/w4.

Personal Allowances Worksheet (Keep for your records.)

A Enter "1" for **yourself** if no one else can claim you as a dependent . . . . **A** _____

B Enter "1" if: { • You're single and have only one job; or
• You're married, have only one job, and your spouse doesn't work; or
• Your wages from a second job or your spouse's wages (or the total of both) are $1,500 or less. } . . . **B** _____

C Enter "1" for your **spouse**. But, you may choose to enter "-0-" if you are married and have either a working spouse or more than one job. (Entering "-0-" may help you avoid having too little tax withheld.) . . . . **C** _____

D Enter number of **dependents** (other than your spouse or yourself) you will claim on your tax return . . . . **D** _____

E Enter "1" if you will file as **head of household** on your tax return (see conditions under **Head of household** above) . . **E** _____

F Enter "1" if you have at least $2,000 of **child or dependent care expenses** for which you plan to claim a credit . . **F** _____

(**Note:** Do **not** include child support payments. See Pub. 503, Child and Dependent Care Expenses, for details.)

G **Child Tax Credit** (including additional child tax credit). See Pub. 972, Child Tax Credit, for more information.

• If your total income will be less than $70,000 ($100,000 if married), enter "2" for each eligible child; then **less** "1" if you have two to four eligible children or **less** "2" if you have five or more eligible children.

• If your total income will be between $70,000 and $84,000 ($100,000 and $119,000 if married), enter "1" for each eligible child. **G** _____

H Add lines A through G and enter total here. (**Note:** This may be different from the number of exemptions you claim on your tax return.) ▶ **H** _____

For accuracy, complete all worksheets that apply. {
• If you plan to **itemize** or **claim adjustments to income** and want to reduce your withholding, see the **Deductions and Adjustments Worksheet** on page 2.

• If you are **single and have more than one job** or are **married and you and your spouse both work** and the combined earnings from all jobs exceed $50,000 ($20,000 if married), see the **Two-Earners/Multiple Jobs Worksheet** on page 2 to avoid having too little tax withheld.

• If **neither** of the above situations applies, **stop here** and enter the number from line H on line 5 of Form W-4 below.
}

-------- **Separate here and give Form W-4 to your employer. Keep the top part for your records.** --------

Form **W-4** Department of the Treasury Internal Revenue Service	**Employee's Withholding Allowance Certificate** ▶ Whether you are entitled to claim a certain number of allowances or exemption from withholding is subject to review by the IRS. Your employer may be required to send a copy of this form to the IRS.	OMB No. 1545-0074 20**17**

1 Your first name and middle initial	Last name	**2** Your social security number

Home address (number and street or rural route)	**3** ☐ Single ☐ Married ☐ Married, but withhold at higher Single rate. **Note:** If married, but legally separated, or spouse is a nonresident alien, check the "Single" box.
City or town, state, and ZIP code	**4** If your last name differs from that shown on your social security card, check here. You must call 1-800-772-1213 for a replacement card. ▶ ☐

5 Total number of allowances you are claiming (from line **H** above **or** from the applicable worksheet on page 2) **5** _____

6 Additional amount, if any, you want withheld from each paycheck **6** $_____

7 I claim exemption from withholding for 2017, and I certify that I meet **both** of the following conditions for exemption.

• Last year I had a right to a refund of **all** federal income tax withheld because I had **no** tax liability, **and**

• This year I expect a refund of **all** federal income tax withheld because I expect to have **no** tax liability.

If you meet both conditions, write "Exempt" here . . . . ▶ **7** _____

Under penalties of perjury, I declare that I have examined this certificate and, to the best of my knowledge and belief, it is true, correct, and complete.

Employee's signature
(This form is not valid unless you sign it.) ▶ _____ Date ▶ _____

8 Employer's name and address (Employer: Complete lines 8 and 10 only if sending to the IRS.)	**9** Office code (optional)	**10** Employer identification number (EIN)

For Privacy Act and Paperwork Reduction Act Notice, see page 2. Cat. No. 10220Q Form **W-4** (2017)

164

Form W-4 (2017)

Purpose. Complete Form W-4 so that your employer can withhold the correct federal income tax from your pay. Consider completing a new Form W-4 each year and when your personal or financial situation changes.

Exemption from withholding. If you are exempt, complete only lines 1, 2, 3, 4, and 7 and sign the form to validate it. Your exemption for 2017 expires February 15, 2018. See Pub. 505, Tax Withholding and Estimated Tax.

Note: If another person can claim you as a dependent on his or her tax return, you can't claim exemption from withholding if your total income exceeds $1,050 and includes more than $350 of unearned income (for example, interest and dividends).

Exceptions. An employee may be able to claim exemption from withholding even if the employee is a dependent, if the employee:
• Is age 65 or older,
• Is blind, or
• Will claim adjustments to income; tax credits; or itemized deductions, on his or her tax return.

The exceptions don't apply to supplemental wages greater than $1,000,000.

Basic instructions. If you aren't exempt, complete the **Personal Allowances Worksheet** below. The worksheets on page 2 further adjust your withholding allowances based on itemized deductions, certain credits, adjustments to income, or two-earners/multiple jobs situations.

Complete all worksheets that apply. However, you may claim fewer (or zero) allowances. For regular wages, withholding must be based on allowances you claimed and may not be a flat amount or percentage of wages.

Head of household. Generally, you can claim head of household filing status on your tax return only if you are unmarried and pay more than 50% of the costs of keeping up a home for yourself and your dependent(s) or other qualifying individuals. See Pub. 501, Exemptions, Standard Deduction, and Filing Information, for information.

Tax credits. You can take projected tax credits into account in figuring your allowable number of withholding allowances. Credits for child or dependent care expenses and the child tax credit may be claimed using the **Personal Allowances Worksheet** below. See Pub. 505 for information on converting your other credits into withholding allowances.

Nonwage income. If you have a large amount of nonwage income, such as interest or dividends, consider making estimated tax payments using Form 1040-ES, Estimated Tax for Individuals. Otherwise, you may owe additional tax. If you have pension or annuity income, see Pub. 505 to find out if you should adjust your withholding on Form W-4 or W-4P.

Two earners or multiple jobs. If you have a working spouse or more than one job, figure the total number of allowances you are entitled to claim on all jobs using worksheets from only one Form W-4. Your withholding usually will be most accurate when all allowances are claimed on the Form W-4 for the highest paying job and zero allowances are claimed on the others. See Pub. 505 for details.

Nonresident alien. If you are a nonresident alien, see Notice 1392, Supplemental Form W-4 Instructions for Nonresident Aliens, before completing this form.

Check your withholding. After your Form W-4 takes effect, use Pub. 505 to see how the amount you are having withheld compares to your projected total tax for 2017. See Pub. 505, especially if your earnings exceed $130,000 (Single) or $180,000 (Married).

Future developments. Information about any future developments affecting Form W-4 (such as legislation enacted after we release it) will be posted at www.irs.gov/w4.

Personal Allowances Worksheet (Keep for your records.)

A Enter "1" for **yourself** if no one else can claim you as a dependent . . . . **A** _____

B Enter "1" if:
• You're single and have only one job; or
• You're married, have only one job, and your spouse doesn't work; or
• Your wages from a second job or your spouse's wages (or the total of both) are $1,500 or less. **B** _____

C Enter "1" for your **spouse**. But, you may choose to enter "-0-" if you are married and have either a working spouse or more than one job. (Entering "-0-" may help you avoid having too little tax withheld.) . . . **C** _____

D Enter number of **dependents** (other than your spouse or yourself) you will claim on your tax return . . . **D** _____

E Enter "1" if you will file as **head of household** on your tax return (see conditions under **Head of household** above) . . **E** _____

F Enter "1" if you have at least $2,000 of **child or dependent care expenses** for which you plan to claim a credit **F** _____
(**Note:** Do **not** include child support payments. See Pub. 503, Child and Dependent Care Expenses, for details.)

G **Child Tax Credit** (including additional child tax credit). See Pub. 972, Child Tax Credit, for more information.
• If your total income will be less than $70,000 ($100,000 if married), enter "2" for each eligible child; then **less** "1" if you have two to four eligible children or **less** "2" if you have five or more eligible children.
• If your total income will be between $70,000 and $84,000 ($100,000 and $119,000 if married), enter "1" for each eligible child. **G** _____

H Add lines A through G and enter total here. (**Note:** This may be different from the number of exemptions you claim on your tax return.) ▶ **H** _____

For accuracy, complete all worksheets that apply.
• If you plan to **itemize** or **claim adjustments to income** and want to reduce your withholding, see the **Deductions and Adjustments Worksheet** on page 2.
• If you are **single and have more than one job** or are **married and you and your spouse both work** and the combined earnings from all jobs exceed $50,000 ($20,000 if married), see the **Two-Earners/Multiple Jobs Worksheet** on page 2 to avoid having too little tax withheld.
• If **neither** of the above situations applies, **stop here** and enter the number from line H on line 5 of Form W-4 below.

---------------- Separate here and give Form W-4 to your employer. Keep the top part for your records. ----------------

Form W-4 — Employee's Withholding Allowance Certificate

Department of the Treasury
Internal Revenue Service

▶ Whether you are entitled to claim a certain number of allowances or exemption from withholding is subject to review by the IRS. Your employer may be required to send a copy of this form to the IRS.

OMB No. 1545-0074

2017

1 Your first name and middle initial	Last name	2 Your social security number

Home address (number and street or rural route)	3 ☐ Single ☐ Married ☐ Married, but withhold at higher Single rate.
	Note: If married, but legally separated, or spouse is a nonresident alien, check the "Single" box.
City or town, state, and ZIP code	4 If your last name differs from that shown on your social security card, check here. You must call 1-800-772-1213 for a replacement card. ▶ ☐

5 Total number of allowances you are claiming (from line **H** above **or** from the applicable worksheet on page 2) **5** _____

6 Additional amount, if any, you want withheld from each paycheck . . . . **6** $ _____

7 I claim exemption from withholding for 2017, and I certify that I meet **both** of the following conditions for exemption.
• Last year I had a right to a refund of **all** federal income tax withheld because I had **no** tax liability, **and**
• This year I expect a refund of **all** federal income tax withheld because I expect to have **no** tax liability.
If you meet both conditions, write "Exempt" here . . . . ▶ **7** _____

Under penalties of perjury, I declare that I have examined this certificate and, to the best of my knowledge and belief, it is true, correct, and complete.

Employee's signature
(This form is not valid unless you sign it.) ▶ _____ Date ▶ _____

8 Employer's name and address (Employer: Complete lines 8 and 10 only if sending to the IRS.)	9 Office code (optional)	10 Employer identification number (EIN)

For Privacy Act and Paperwork Reduction Act Notice, see page 2.   Cat. No. 10220Q   Form **W-4** (2017)

AUTISM WORKS NOW Workplace Paperwork

9 FORM I-9

Employment Eligibility Verification
Department of Homeland Security
U.S. Citizenship and Immigration Services

USCIS
Form I-9
OMB No. 1615-0047
Expires 08/31/2019

▶ **START HERE:** Read instructions carefully before completing this form. The instructions must be available, either in paper or electronically, during completion of this form. Employers are liable for errors in the completion of this form.

ANTI-DISCRIMINATION NOTICE: It is illegal to discriminate against work-authorized individuals. Employers **CANNOT** specify which document(s) an employee may present to establish employment authorization and identity. The refusal to hire or continue to employ an individual because the documentation presented has a future expiration date may also constitute illegal discrimination.

Section 1. Employee Information and Attestation *(Employees must complete and sign Section 1 of Form I-9 no later than the first day of employment, but not before accepting a job offer.)*

Last Name *(Family Name)*	First Name *(Given Name)*		Middle Initial	Other Last Names Used *(if any)*
Address *(Street Number and Name)*	Apt. Number	City or Town	State	ZIP Code
Date of Birth *(mm/dd/yyyy)*	U.S. Social Security Number	Employee's E-mail Address		Employee's Telephone Number

I am aware that federal law provides for imprisonment and/or fines for false statements or use of false documents in connection with the completion of this form.

I attest, under penalty of perjury, that I am (check one of the following boxes):

☐ 1. A citizen of the United States

☐ 2. A noncitizen national of the United States *(See instructions)*

☐ 3. A lawful permanent resident   (Alien Registration Number/USCIS Number): _____

☐ 4. An alien authorized to work   until (expiration date, if applicable, mm/dd/yyyy): _____
    Some aliens may write "N/A" in the expiration date field. *(See instructions)*

Aliens authorized to work must provide only one of the following document numbers to complete Form I-9:
An Alien Registration Number/USCIS Number OR Form I-94 Admission Number OR Foreign Passport Number.

1. Alien Registration Number/USCIS Number: _____
                    OR
2. Form I-94 Admission Number: _____
                    OR
3. Foreign Passport Number: _____
    Country of Issuance: _____

QR Code - Section 1
Do Not Write In This Space

Signature of Employee	Today's Date *(mm/dd/yyyy)*

Preparer and/or Translator Certification (check one):

☐ I did not use a preparer or translator.   ☐ A preparer(s) and/or translator(s) assisted the employee in completing Section 1.
(Fields below must be completed and signed when preparers and/or translators assist an employee in completing Section 1.)

I attest, under penalty of perjury, that I have assisted in the completion of Section 1 of this form and that to the best of my knowledge the information is true and correct.

Signature of Preparer or Translator	Today's Date *(mm/dd/yyyy)*
Last Name *(Family Name)*	First Name *(Given Name)*		
Address *(Street Number and Name)*	City or Town	State	ZIP Code

🛑 *Employer Completes Next Page* 🛑

Form I-9 11/14/2016 N

Page 1 of 3

Employment Eligibility Verification
Department of Homeland Security
U.S. Citizenship and Immigration Services

USCIS
Form I-9
OMB No. 1615-0047
Expires 08/31/2019

Section 2. Employer or Authorized Representative Review and Verification

(Employers or their authorized representative must complete and sign Section 2 within 3 business days of the employee's first day of employment. You must physically examine one document from List A OR a combination of one document from List B and one document from List C as listed on the "Lists of Acceptable Documents.")

Employee Info from Section 1	Last Name *(Family Name)*	First Name *(Given Name)*	M.I.	Citizenship/Immigration Status

List A Identity and Employment Authorization	OR	List B Identity	AND	List C Employment Authorization
Document Title		Document Title		Document Title
Issuing Authority		Issuing Authority		Issuing Authority
Document Number		Document Number		Document Number
Expiration Date *(if any)(mm/dd/yyyy)*		Expiration Date *(if any)(mm/dd/yyyy)*		Expiration Date *(if any)(mm/dd/yyyy)*
Document Title				
Issuing Authority		Additional Information		QR Code - Sections 2 & 3 Do Not Write In This Space
Document Number				
Expiration Date *(if any)(mm/dd/yyyy)*				
Document Title				
Issuing Authority				
Document Number				
Expiration Date *(if any)(mm/dd/yyyy)*				

Certification: I attest, under penalty of perjury, that (1) I have examined the document(s) presented by the above-named employee, (2) the above-listed document(s) appear to be genuine and to relate to the employee named, and (3) to the best of my knowledge the employee is authorized to work in the United States.

The employee's first day of employment *(mm/dd/yyyy)*: _____ *(See instructions for exemptions)*

Signature of Employer or Authorized Representative	Today's Date *(mm/dd/yyyy)*	Title of Employer or Authorized Representative
Last Name of Employer or Authorized Representative	First Name of Employer or Authorized Representative	Employer's Business or Organization Name

Employer's Business or Organization Address (Street Number and Name)	City or Town	State	ZIP Code

Section 3. Reverification and Rehires *(To be completed and signed by employer or authorized representative.)*

A. New Name *(if applicable)*			B. Date of Rehire *(if applicable)*
Last Name *(Family Name)*	First Name *(Given Name)*	Middle Initial	Date *(mm/dd/yyyy)*

C. If the employee's previous grant of employment authorization has expired, provide the information for the document or receipt that establishes continuing employment authorization in the space provided below.

Document Title	Document Number	Expiration Date *(if any) (mm/dd/yyyy)*

I attest, under penalty of perjury, that to the best of my knowledge, this employee is authorized to work in the United States, and if the employee presented document(s), the document(s) I have examined appear to be genuine and to relate to the individual.

Signature of Employer or Authorized Representative	Today's Date *(mm/dd/yyyy)*	Name of Employer or Authorized Representative

★

LISTS OF ACCEPTABLE DOCUMENTS
All documents must be UNEXPIRED

Employees may present one selection from List A
or a combination of one selection from List B and one selection from List C.

LIST A		LIST B		LIST C
Documents that Establish Both Identity and Employment Authorization	OR	**Documents that Establish Identity**	AND	**Documents that Establish Employment Authorization**
1. U.S. Passport or U.S. Passport Card		1. Driver's license or ID card issued by a State or outlying possession of the United States provided it contains a photograph or information such as name, date of birth, gender, height, eye color, and address		1. A Social Security Account Number card, unless the card includes one of the following restrictions: (1) NOT VALID FOR EMPLOYMENT (2) VALID FOR WORK ONLY WITH INS AUTHORIZATION (3) VALID FOR WORK ONLY WITH DHS AUTHORIZATION
2. Permanent Resident Card or Alien Registration Receipt Card (Form I-551)				
3. Foreign passport that contains a temporary I-551 stamp or temporary I-551 printed notation on a machine-readable immigrant visa		2. ID card issued by federal, state or local government agencies or entities, provided it contains a photograph or information such as name, date of birth, gender, height, eye color, and address		
4. Employment Authorization Document that contains a photograph (Form I-766)		3. School ID card with a photograph		2. Certification of Birth Abroad issued by the Department of State (Form FS-545)
5. For a nonimmigrant alien authorized to work for a specific employer because of his or her status: a. Foreign passport; and b. Form I-94 or Form I-94A that has the following: (1) The same name as the passport; and (2) An endorsement of the alien's nonimmigrant status as long as that period of endorsement has not yet expired and the proposed employment is not in conflict with any restrictions or limitations identified on the form.		4. Voter's registration card		3. Certification of Report of Birth issued by the Department of State (Form DS-1350)
		5. U.S. Military card or draft record		4. Original or certified copy of birth certificate issued by a State, county, municipal authority, or territory of the United States bearing an official seal
		6. Military dependent's ID card		
		7. U.S. Coast Guard Merchant Mariner Card		5. Native American tribal document
		8. Native American tribal document		6. U.S. Citizen ID Card (Form I-197)
		9. Driver's license issued by a Canadian government authority		7. Identification Card for Use of Resident Citizen in the United States (Form I-179)
		For persons under age 18 who are unable to present a document listed above:		8. Employment authorization document issued by the Department of Homeland Security
6. Passport from the Federated States of Micronesia (FSM) or the Republic of the Marshall Islands (RMI) with Form I-94 or Form I-94A indicating nonimmigrant admission under the Compact of Free Association Between the United States and the FSM or RMI		10. School record or report card 11. Clinic, doctor, or hospital record 12. Day-care or nursery school record		

Examples of many of these documents appear in Part 8 of the Handbook for Employers (M-274).

Refer to the instructions for more information about acceptable receipts.

★

10 RESUME WORKSHEET EXAMPLE

Your Name Here

Telephone Number_____

Email Address_____

SUMMARY

Example: Energetic, reliable, and hard-working high school graduate who is looking for a full-time or part-time job

PROFESSIONAL EXPERIENCE
Name of Company, City, State   **Year started to Present**

Job Title

- *Responsibilities and Accomplishments*
- *Responsibilities and Accomplishments*

Name of Company, City, State   **Year started to year ended**

Job Title

- *Responsibilities and Accomplishments*
- *Responsibilities and Accomplishments*

EDUCATION
College Degree _____

Diploma _____

ACCOMPLISHMENTS/HONORS/AWARDS

-
-

★

SKILLS

- *Software proficiency*
- *Typing speed*
- *Special training*

INTERESTS AND HOBBIES

- *Interest/hobby*
- *Interest/hobby*

★

AUTISM WORKS NOW Workplace Paperwork

RESUME WORKSHEET

Name: _____

Telephone Number _____

Email Address _____

SUMMARY

_____

_____

PROFESSIONAL EXPERIENCE
Name of Company, City, State   **Year started to Present**

_____

_____

Job Title:_____

- *Responsibilities and Accomplishments:* _____
- *Responsibilities and Accomplishments:* _____

Name of Company, City, State   **Year started to year ended**

_____

_____

Job Title: _____

- *Responsibilities and Accomplishments:* _____
- *Responsibilities and Accomplishments:* _____

EDUCATION
Diploma/College Degree _____

Certificates _____

ACCOMPLISHMENTS/HONORS/AWARDS

_____

_____

SKILLS

- *Software proficiency* _____
- *Typing speed* _____
- *Special training* _____

INTERESTS AND HOBBIES

- *Interest/hobby* _____
- *Interest/hobby* _____

AUTISM WORKS NOW Roundtable Discussion

11 YOUR WEEK WORKSHEET—
WHAT HAPPENED WITH YOU?

Name: _____

Date: _____

Where did you go?

_____

_____

_____

When did you go?

_____

_____

_____

Who went with you?

_____

_____

_____

What did you do?

_____

_____

_____

What was your favorite part of the activity?

_____

_____

_____

AUTISM WORKS NOW Roundtable Discussion

YOUR WEEK WORKSHEET— INTERVIEW YOUR PARTNER

Name: _____

Name of Partner: _____

Date: _____

ASK YOUR PARTNER THESE QUESTIONS:

Where did you go?

_____

_____

_____

When did you go?

_____

_____

_____

Who went with you?

_____

_____

_____

What did you do?

_____

_____

_____

What was your favorite part of the activity?

_____

_____

_____

AUTISM WORKS NOW Roundtable Discussion

12 ICEBREAKER WORKSHEET

Name: _____

Date: _____

Today's Icebreaker: _____

Candidate Name   Answer

_____   _____

_____   _____

_____   _____

_____   _____

_____   _____

_____   _____

_____   _____

_____   _____

_____   _____

_____   _____

_____   _____

_____   _____

_____   _____

_____   _____

13 AWN INCREDIBLE 5-POINT GROUP CHECK IN SCALE

1
I am really glad to be here.
I will participate and I may even be able to help others.

2
I am glad to be here and I will participate.

3
I'm here. I might or might not participate.

4
I'm here. I will not participate but I will not disrupt.

5
I will not participate and I may disrupt if I have to stay.

AUTISM WORKS NOW Roundtable Discussion

14 AWN INCREDIBLE 5-POINT STRESS METER

_____'s Stress Meter

	What my Face Looks Like	How My Body Feels	What I Can Do to Calm Down
5			
4			
3			
2			No Action Needed
1			No Action Needed

★

15 AWN SODA CHART

Stop Observe Deliberate Act

THINK BEFORE YOU ACT WITH

Before making a decision ...

 STOP

 OBSERVE

 DELIBERATE

 ACT

★

178

16 MINDFULNESS BREATHING EXERCISE

MINDFULNESS

Definition of mindfulness

Mindfulness is being completely in touch with and aware of the present moment and taking a non-judgmental approach to your inner experience. A mindful approach to one's inner experience is simply viewing "thoughts as thoughts" as opposed to evaluating certain thoughts as positive or negative. The term comes from Eastern spiritual and religious traditions like Zen Buddhism.

How to practice being mindful

Mindfulness is about being completely in touch with the present moment. So often in our lives, we get stuck in our heads, caught up in the anxiety and worries of daily life. This exercise will introduce you to mindfulness and should be helpful in getting you "out of your head" and in touch with the present moment.

It is important to practice this exercise when you are not overly stressed out or anxious. It's similar to the experience of learning to drive a car. You don't begin driving on a busy freeway during rush hour. You start in an empty parking lot or on the streets in your neighborhood when there is not a lot of activity or many cars on the road. The same process goes for the practice of mindfulness.

Remember, it is normal for your mind to wander during this exercise, so don't get discouraged. For times like this, it may be useful to think of mindfulness in this way: if your mind wanders away from your breath one hundred times, mindfulness is about bringing your attention back to the present moment a hundred and one times.

Proper breathing

Before you try your mindful breathing exercise, it is useful to practice proper breathing. This may sound silly, but many people don"t breathe properly, which can cause them to become stressed and anxious.

Over time, people forget how to breathe properly and instead take short and shallow breaths, which can increase stress and anxiety. It is never too late to "re-learn" how to breathe to avoid becoming stressed.

Natural breathing involves your diaphragm, a large muscle in your abdomen. When you breathe in, your belly should expand. When you breathe out, your belly should fall.

★

MINDFULNESS BREATHING EXERCISE

Find a comfortable position in a quiet place. Sit in a position that is comfortable enough for you to fully relax your body and completely immerse yourself into your breathing. It should also be quiet enough for you to hear your own breathing.

Begin from a physically relaxed place. Release the thoughts and the stresses from your mind and just let your mind relax. These may be things that have occurred today or have been happening in your life for a while. Don't breathe from a "stressed" place. You may become distracted and try to change it.

Set an alarm. It will be easier for you to let go and relax into your breathing if you have a set end time. Also, if you fall asleep, the alarm will wake you so you don't oversleep and miss an appointment.

Relax your shoulders. Before you begin, relax your shoulders and let them fall. They shouldn't rise and fall as you breathe.

Breathe from your diaphragm. Breathe deeply. Your belly should rise with every inbreath and fall with every outbreath. This is the natural way of breathing.

Notice your breathing. Once you've relaxed your breathing, don't try to change it. Eventually, you will find yourself feeling a "oneness" with your breathing.

Focus your attention on your breathing. Let the awareness of your breath keep you anchored in the present moment. As your thoughts come and go, as physical sensations arise, or as noises happen in your environment, return your focus to back to your breathing.

Don't judge yourself when your mind wanders. This is completely normal. Instead, congratulate yourself for noticing that your mind's focus has shifted and gently redirect your attention back to your breathing.

Continue as long as you would like! Three to ten minutes is a good amount of time to practice mindfulness breathing.

Make this a habit. Practice this exercise at least once a day or when you feel the need to destress.

- For more information, click on UCLA Mindfulness Awareness Research Center at http://marc.ucla.edu/body.cfm?id=2http://marc.ucla.edu/mindful-meditations

- For additional meditations from the MARC, click on Free Guided Meditations at http://marc.ucla.edu/mindful-meditations

AUTISM WORKS NOW Roundtable Discussion

17 STRESS MANAGEMENT WORKSHEET

Name: _____

When did you experience stress?

   Date and Time of day: _____

   What happened before: _____

   _____

   What happened after: _____

   _____

What level was your stress using the Incredible 5-Point Scale? *Check one*

Low Stress(1 – 2)	**Medium Stress (3)**	**High Stress (4 – 5)**
Not much	*Felt stressed but didn't lose my temper*	*Had a meltdown or lost my temper*
☐	☐	☐

How did your body react?

   Face _____

   Jaws _____

   Forehead _____

   Cheeks _____

   Ears _____

   Eyes _____

   Throat _____

   Chest _____

   Heart _____

   Arms/Hands _____

   Feet/Legs _____

What did you do to manage your stress?

- ☐ I took deep breaths
- ☐ I visualized something to calm myself down
- ☐ I took a walk outside to clear my head
- ☐ Something else: _____

What was the outcome?

- ☐ It went well and I wouldn't change anything.
- ☐ It went OK, but I want to change how I react next time.
- ☐ It didn't go well and I need to change how I react next time.

If I want a different outcome next time, what could I do differently?

_____

_____

★

18 TIME MANAGEMENT WORKSHEET

Appointment time	____:____
Subtract 15 minutes from your appointment time	____: 15
THIS IS YOUR ARRIVAL TIME	____:____
Subtract travel time *(confirm on Google Maps)*	____:____
Subtract 20 minutes for parking and finding location	____: 20
THIS IS YOUR DEPARTURE TIME	____:____
Subtract total preparation time from Preparation Checklist below	____:____ *
THIS IS WHEN YOU START GETTING READY	____:____

PREPARATION CHECKLIST
Make a list of things you must do before you leave.
Estimate the amount of time needed to complete each item and add
the total number of minutes. Enter above at the line with the *.

*Number of minutes
to complete*

Shower/shave/put on make up	_____
Get dressed	_____
Other:	_____
Other:	_____
Other:	_____
Other:	_____
Other:	_____
Total Preparation Time (enter above)	_____ *

19 GETTING ORGANIZED WITH GOOGLE: GMAIL FORMATTING OPTIONS

TO/RECIPIENTS: TOP SECTION

TO: Person you are sending the email to
CC: Copy of email will be sent and original recipient will know it's been copied
BCC: Copy email will be sent but original recipient won't know it's been copied

SUBJECT: MIDDLE SECTION

SUBJECT: Title or subject of your email

BOTTOM SECTION

Text of your email

FORMATTING OPTIONS: CLICK ON *A* (bottom left side of screen)

FONTS: 11 options

1. Comic Sans
2. Fixed Width
3. Garamond
4. Georgia
5. arrow
6. San Serif
7. Serif
8. Tahoma
9. Trebuchet MS

10. Veranda

11. Wide

TEXT SIZE—TT: 4 options
small
normal

large

huge

B	*I*	<u>U</u>	A
Bold	*Italics*	<u>Underline</u>	Text Highlight

Justify: 3 options

Left	Center	Right

1. Numbered list:

• Bulleted list:

Indent: 2 options

⇨ Indent right

Indent left ⇦

Quotations

Undo

Tx

★

AUTISM WORKS NOW Prepare and Practice

GETTING ORGANIZED WITH GOOGLE: GOOGLE CONTACT SPREADSHEET

Name: _____

Company: _____

Email: _____

Office Phone #: _____

Mobile Phone #: _____

Address: _____

Birthday: _____

Website: _____

Notes *(include information about where did you meet the person:*

_____

_____

_____

20 DRESS FOR SUCCESS: MEN'S MEASUREMENT WORKSHEET

HOW TO MEASURE: REMEMBER TO KEEP THE TAPE LOOSE

NECK   _____ Measure around middle of neck at Adam's apple

CHEST   _____ Measure under arms around the fullest part of chest and relax arms at your side

WAIST   _____ Measure around natural waistline

HIPS   _____ Measure around the fullest part of your hips and buttocks

INSEAM   _____ Measure from top of your inner thigh down to bottom of ankle

ARM LENGTH   _____ Bend elbow 90 degrees and place hand on hip
Hold tape at center of back of your neck
Measure across shoulder down to elbow and down to - waist

HEIGHT   _____ Measure from top of head to floor while standing straight

DRESS FOR SUCCESS: WOMEN'S MEASUREMENT WORKSHEET

HOW TO MEASURE: REMEMBER TO KEEP THE TAPE LOOSE

NECK   _____ Measure around middle of neck at Adam's apple

CHEST   _____ Measure under arms around the fullest part of chest and relax arms at your side

WAIST   _____ Measure around natural waistline

HIPS   _____ Measure around the fullest part of your hips and buttocks

INSEAM   _____ Measure from top of your inner thigh down to bottom of ankle

ARM LENGTH _____ Bend elbow 90 degrees and place hand on hip
Hold tape at center of back of your neck
Measure across shoulder down to elbow and down to - waist

HEIGHT   _____ Measure from top of head to floor while standing straight

DRESS HEIGHT _____ Measure from nape of neck to desired length

SKIRT HEIGHT _____ Measure from middle of waist to desired length

AUTISM WORKS NOW Prepare and Practice

21 INTERVIEW ESSENTIALS: INTERVIEW PREP CHECKLIST

Name: _____

BEFORE INTERVIEW (1–2 DAYS)

- Research the company
  - ○ What does the company do, produce, or create?
  - ○ How long has the company been in business?
  - ○ Who are the senior managers (CEO, COO, President)?
- Prepare 5 questions to ask the interviewer based on your research
- Prepare answers to list of **10 Frequently Asked Interview Questions**
- Practice your introduction to the receptionist and greeting to interviewer
- Prepare and practice your elevator pitch
- Complete the **Day/Night Before Checklist** and **Transportation Checklist**
- Complete the **Time Management Worksheet**

DURING INTERVIEW (BEFORE MEETING WITH INTERVIEWER)

- Use the **AWN Incredible 5-Point Check In Scale** to assess your internal state
- Stay relaxed using visualization and mindful breathing
- Smile and say hello when meeting anyone that walks by
- Turn your phone off or to silent

★

DURING INTERVIEW (WHILE MEETING WITH INTERVIEWER)

- Use a firm handshake
- Listen to interviewer's questions and don't speak until they are done talking
- Focus your answers on your strengths and transferrable skills
- Stay positive: don't say anything negative about former employers or coworkers
- Use appropriate language: don't use slang
- Keep discussion on benefits you'll bring to employer and your skills related to job
- Do not make up answers or say anything that isn't true

END OF INTERVIEW

- Ask the interviewer the date a decision will be made
- Ask for the interviewer's business card

FOLLOW-UP

- Send a thank you email or mail a written note within 1 day of the interview
- If no word, email or call on the date that the interviewer said a decision would be made
- Complete **Interview Reflection Checklist** to identify ways to improve in next interview

AUTISM WORKS NOW Prepare and Practice

INTERVIEW ESSENTIALS: DAY/ NIGHT BEFORE CHECKLIST

Check the circle next to the item when it is completed.

- ☐ On my calendar, I entered an event with a name, location and person I'm meeting into my Google Calendar

- ☐ I picked out my clothes and shoes

- ☐ I checked that my clothes and shoes are clean and don't need repairs

- ☐ I washed my clothes and cleaned my shoes if they needed cleaning

- ☐ I charged my phone

- ☐ I gathered the following items for my appointment:

    - ☐ Resume

    - ☐ References

    - ☐ Paperwork: _____

    - ☐ Book(s): _____

    - ☐ Notebook

- ☐ I put all the items in a folder or bag

- ☐ I placed the folder or bag where I can easily see it when I leave

- ☐ I need to eat breakfast, lunch, or dinner before I leave   **Yes   No**

STOP HERE
If yes:

- ☐ I have the food items I need to make my meal   **Yes   No**

STOP HERE
If no:

- ☐ I made a list of the food items I need to buy

- ☐ I went grocery shopping the afternoon before my appointment

- ☐ I have completed the Transportation Checklist (below)

INTERVIEW ESSENTIALS: TRANSPORTATION CHECKLIST

- ☐ I am traveling by car
    - ☐ I have enough gas in my car to get home and back
    - ☐ I know where I will park
    - ☐ I have money for garage parking or change for the meter
- ☐ I am traveling by public transportation
    - ☐ I know which bus route to take
    - ☐ I know which bus stop to stop and get on
    - ☐ I know the bus schedule
    - ☐ I have money for bus fare
- ☐ I'm getting a ride or taking Access
- ☐ I have confirmed the day and time with my driver or pickup time with Access at least one day to pickup

INTERVIEW ESSENTIALS: 10 FREQUENTLY ASKED INTERVIEW QUESTIONS

1. Can you tell me about yourself?

2. What are your key strengths/skills?

3. What are your weaknesses?

4. What kind of environment would you like to work in?

5. If I were to call your references, what would they say about you?

6. When reading the job description, what interested you in this position?

7. Can you give me an example of a difficult situation and how you dealt with it?

8. What are your career goals?

9. What do you know about the organization?

10. Why should we hire you?

INTERVIEW ESSENTIALS: ELEVATOR PITCH OVERVIEW

Imagine, you're scheduled for interview for a job that you really want. Upon your arrival, you're instructed to take the elevator to the HR Department on the top floor. At the next stop, to your great surprise, the doors open and the President of the company enters the elevator! Right now, you need a quick and easy way to introduce yourself and summarize how your skill sets are a good match for the organization.

An "Elevator Pitch" is a prepared introduction of 60 seconds or less that summarizes who you are, what you do, and how you can benefit an employer. Your pitch can be used at networking events and social gatherings. It can also be used as the foundation of an introductory email, a cover letter, or a social media profile.

An effective elevator pitch answers these three questions:

- What have you done and what can you do?

  o Include any awards, recognitions, and certifications that you've received as well as transferable work skills and areas of strength.

  o If you are in school, include information on your major, clubs memberships, people you admire, and favorite subjects.

  o Words that are good for explaining what you can do are:

    – adept at...

    – proficient in...

    – accomplished...

    – expertise in...

    – savvy...

- What are your best skills and abilities?

  o Be specific on what you do best.

  o Consider areas where are you most confident.

★

- o Focus on positive feedback that you've received about your work.
- o Words that are good for explaining your skills are:
  - have a knack for...
  - talented at...
  - effective at...
- What would you like to do?
  - o You need to communicate what you want so the person will know how to help you. Do you:
    - want help with a job reference?
    - want to schedule an informational interview?
    - need to do well in an interview?
  - o Words to use that communicate what your needs are:
    - gain exposure to the industry...
    - hoping to find a role in...
    - suggestions as to how I can...
    - looking for opportunities to develop my skills...
    - insight on how I can apply...
- What type of job do you want?
  - o Explain what motivates you and why the work is meaningful to you outside of the paycheck.
  - o Ask yourself:
    - Who do I want to help or inspire?
    - Who benefits from my work?
    - Why do I enjoy this line of work?
  - o Words that are good for explaining why you want this type of job:
    - because...
    - on behalf of...
    - I'm inspired by...
    - I believe...

The delivery of your elevator pitch might feel awkward at first, but with practice, you will feel more confident and it will feel more natural and authentic. So, practice—a lot. And remember when speaking, a smile on your face will put a smile in your voice.

The following are ways you can practice and improve your Elevator Pitch.

- Practice in front of a mirror to watch your facial expressions.

- Record your speech with your phone and replay later to hear how you sound.

- Videotape yourself with your phone so you can replay later to see how you look.

- Practice saying your speech to someone you respect and ask for their feedback.

ELEVATOR PITCH SAMPLES

15 seconds

I am seeking an internship in the restaurant industry so I can start my career as a chef. My eventual career goal is to become a fully-qualified and experienced professional restaurateur with the longer-term aspiration of running my own business.

30 seconds

I am a sophomore at the ABC High School, and I am interested in a career as an engineer. As a member of the school Robotics Club, I worked as part of a team to design and build several robots. I also completed an internship at a robotic design firm where I assisted in multiple departments including engineering, research and development, marketing, and distribution.

60 seconds

I believe that my background and experience have provided me with the skills necessary to excel in the role as a production assistant. I have almost two years of television production experience from my internship at The X Show, where I was exposed to all aspects of TV production. I made such a strong impression the first summer, I was invited back and given a role with more responsibility. I am currently working part time for a production company in an assistant role and I was given an opportunity to help edit several episodes of a show that the company produces. I have a reputation for getting things done and always with a smile. I love working in the TV industry and want to learn and get experience in every way possible.

AUTISM WORKS NOW Prepare and Practice

INTERVIEW ESSENTIALS: ELEVATOR PITCH WORKSHEET

LIST DETAILS ABOUT THE JOB YOU WANT.

Field _____

Position _____

Location _____

Dream Company/Companies _____

_____

LIST YOUR SKILLS, ACCOMPLISHMENTS AND WORK EXPERIENCE THAT IS RELEVANT TO THE JOB.

Use the back of this worksheet if you need more space.

_____

_____

_____

_____

_____

ANSWER THESE QUESTIONS:

Who are you?

_____

_____

_____

_____

_____

_____

What do you do?

_____

_____

_____

_____

_____

_____

What would you like to do?

_____

_____

_____

_____

_____

_____

INTERVIEW ESSENTIALS: INTERVIEW REFLECTION CHECKLIST

	Excellent!	Room for improvement	I need a do-over
Several days before:			
I researched the company	☐	☐	☐
I prepared 5 questions from my research	☐	☐	☐
I prepped answers for 10 frequently asked questions	☐	☐	☐
I practiced my elevator pitch	☐	☐	☐
I checked that my clothes were clean/in good repair	☐	☐	☐
I brought my clothes to dry cleaner (if needed)	☐	☐	☐
The day before:			
I cleaned my nails/got a manicure (gals)	☐	☐	☐
I got a haircut	☐	☐	☐
I practiced my greeting for the receptionist	☐	☐	☐
I practiced my greeting for the interviewer	☐	☐	☐
I added the interview date/time on my Calendar	☐	☐	☐
I estimated time travel on Google Maps	☐	☐	☐
I washed my clothes if they were dirty	☐	☐	☐
I picked up my clothes from dry cleaners (if needed)	☐	☐	☐
The night before:			
I put my resume/references/papers in a bag/folder	☐	☐	☐
I checked that my shoes were clean	☐	☐	☐
I shined/cleaned my shoes (if needed)	☐	☐	☐
I charged my phone	☐	☐	☐
I got 8 hours of sleep	☐	☐	☐

	Excellent!	Room for improvement	I need a do-over

The morning of:

I showered/washed my hair/brushed my teeth

I shaved (guys)/put on make up (gals)

I ate a healthy breakfast or lunch

I did relaxation/stress management exercises

I remembered my bag/folder with my documents

I put money for transportation in my wallet

Before the interview:

I arrived 15 minutes early to the interview

I turned off my cell phone

I said hello to anyone I met

I greeted the receptionist

During the interview

I greeted the interviewer

I shook the interviewer's hand with a firm handshake

I didn't interrupt the interviewer

I stayed on topic

I was relaxed and confident

I smiled

I asked for a business card at the end of the interview

Follow-up:

I sent a thank you email or sent a card in the mail

If I didn't hear back, I called 1 week after the interview

INTERVIEW ESSENTIALS: AWN AMBASSADOR JOB DESCRIPTION

OVERVIEW

The AWN Ambassador's function is to be a representative as a candidate in the Workplace Readiness Workshop at events and conferences where AWN is an exhibitor or is a featured organization. Ambassadors speak to the general public and to potential candidates and their families to share their experience as a candidate in the Workplace Readiness Workshop.

KEY RESPONSIBILITIES

- Attend events and conferences as a representative of AWN

- Answer questions about and share their experience as a candidate in the workshop

- Create and deliver an "elevator pitch" that summarizes the essential elements the workshop

- Maintain proper business casual work attire as the AWN Ambassador

DESIRED SKILLS

- Basic keyboarding abilities preferred but not required

- Knowledge of and experience creating/using word processing documents and spreadsheets preferred but not required

MANDATORY JOB REQUIREMENTS

- Currently enrolled in AWN's Workplace Readiness Workshop

- Arrival no later than thirty (30) minutes prior to start of event

- Ability to attend events and conferences with minimal support

- Ability to lift and/or move up to twenty-five (25) pounds
- Ability to stand, walk, sit, use hands and fingers, and reach with hands and arms
- Ability to adhere to AWN policies and procedures
- Ability to follow instructions in various forms (written, oral, or pictorial)
- Knowledge of basic safety and security procedures

QUALIFICATIONS

To perform this job successfully, an individual must be able to perform each essential duty satisfactorily. The requirements listed above are representative of the knowledge, skill, and/or ability required. Reasonable accommodations may be made to enable individuals with disabilities to perform the essential functions.

RATE OF PAY

$10.50 per hour

22 CONNECTING WITH COWORKERS: MAKING A GOOD FIRST IMPRESSION WHEN STARTING A NEW JOB

As the saying goes, you never get a second chance to make a first impression, and research has proven this to be true. Within the first few seconds of meeting someone, people form assumptions about us based on what we wear, how we speak, and our general attitude. In the workplace, these first impressions can have a long-term impact on our reputation and ultimately determine how successful we are in our career.

Below are ways you can make a positive first impression when starting a new job. Practicing these tips every day will help you develop good workplace habits, which will help solidify your reputation with your coworkers and supervisors.

Keep your attitude positive

The best defense against the daily stressors that we experience in our job is to maintain a positive attitude. Proactively managing our stress helps us stay us calm and focused. Practicing gratitude for job and our loved ones helps us appreciate what we have. Smiling often improves our mood and is appreciated by everyone at work.

Be mindful of formal and informal workplace policies

Become familiar with general office procedures. Learn about the daily office routine and the way that your coworkers like to maintain their environment. Do they like music on or off? Do they like speaking loudly in the hallways, or is it quiet and reserved? As a newcomer, it is your responsibility to observe and adapt to your new work environment as much as possible. *When you don't know something, ask for help. Don't assume, that's when drama starts.*

Get to know your coworkers

Work is not a social gathering place, but you should be friendly with all of your coworkers and remember something about them. After meeting a coworker for the first time, make sure you remember their name. If this is difficult, keep a notepad and write down each name as you learn it along with some distinctive information about the person. Here's an example: *Dave, works in the stockroom. Tall and has dark hair. Likes Anime. Worked here 5 years and a good person to ask questions.*

Try to go to lunch or take a break with a coworker. Try to find a workplace "buddy", someone that knows what's going on and will keep you informed of what is happening at work. But be mindful with whom you associate. The office gossip or troublemaker are not coworkers that are well liked or respected, so if you hang out with one, your coworkers might see you as a gossip or a troublemaker too.

Watch your manners
Say thank you to the people that help you and say please when making a request. Do not tell off-color jokes. Do not get into petty arguments.

Listen carefully
Really listen to what others are saying. Be mindful and attentive to their words. Let your coworkers know that you appreciate and value their opinion. Make eye contact when this is possible. *"We have two ears and one mouth so that we can listen twice as much as we speak."* ~ Epictetus

Watch what you wear
To make a good impression, your clothes need to match the culture of your workplace. Make sure what you wear is clean and in good repair. Follow the company's dress code as much as possible, and don't ever dress too casually. A good rule to follow is: *Don't dress for the job you have. Dress for the job you want.*

Watch what you say and how you say it
The words you say will play a large part in the first impression you make. Be kind, respectful, and truthful when speaking. Don't participate in office gossip. Don't use slang or off-color phrases. Choose your words carefully, because everything you say will be judged. *"When you want to say anything, think like Buddha: If you propose to speak, always ask yourself, is it true, is it necessary, is it kind."*

23 NETWORKING AND LANDING A JOB: INFORMATIONAL INTERVIEW ESSENTIALS

WHAT IS AN INFORMATIONAL INTERVIEW?

An informational interview is a process used to gather career information from professionals. Your goal is not to ask for a job, but rather to gain firsthand information about a specific occupation, job and/or organization from someone with an insider's perspective.

WHY CONDUCT AN INFORMATIONAL INTERVIEW?

An informational interview helps you accomplish several things.

- You make in-person connections with working professionals.

- You obtain a great deal of information about a career of interest and the types of skills you'll need to do the job effectively. All of this data is excellent information to include on a resume and use as the foundation of a social media profile.

- You gain insight into the hidden job market, employment opportunities that are found by referrals and are not advertised or posted.

- You gain confidence in talking with people.

WHAT ARE THE STEPS IN USED IN SCHEDULING AN INFORMATIONAL INTERVIEW?

- Identify a professional that's employed in your field of interest or at a company where you would like to work.

- Contact the person.

  ○ Explain why you are seeking personalized information about their field.

  ○ Ask if you can meet at their worksite for about twenty to thirty minutes.

- Send an email confirmation the day the interview is confirmed.

- Call your contact again no later than 24 hours prior to the start time of your meeting.

- Show up at least 15 minutes early.

- Take notes about important information that you discover during the interview.

★

NETWORKING AND LANDING A JOB: INFORMATIONAL INTERVIEW CONTACT LIST

Below list the prospective professionals that you would like to meet. These can be people that you know, referrals from friends, or professions that you found by browsing the internet.

LEAD 1
Organization _____

Person's Name/Title _____

Business Address _____

Phone Number _____

LEAD 2
Organization _____

Person's Name/Title _____

Business Address _____

Phone Number _____

LEAD 3
Organization _____

Person's Name/Title _____

Business Address _____

Phone Number _____

LEAD 4

Organization _____

Person's Name/Title _____

Business Address _____

Phone Number _____

LEAD 5

Organization _____

Person's Name/Title _____

Business Address _____

Phone Number _____

NETWORKING AND LANDING A JOB: INFORMATIONAL INTERVIEW SCRIPTS AND CORRESPONDENCE

The best chance of success in scheduling an interview is with someone that you already know or have a personal referral for. You can also be successful in scheduling a meeting with someone that you don't have a connection with, but you will need to prepare and practice your introduction before contacting the person.

Below is a sample script that you can use to introduce yourself to someone you haven't met or don't have a referral for. The text in square brackets is where you can revise the script according to your own narrative.

SAMPLE TELEPHONE SCRIPT

[Ms. Jones], my name is [George Michael], and I am enrolled in the Workplace Readiness Workshop with Autism Works Now. This program is helping me to learn the skills I need to get and keep a job. I have learned how to network as part of the program, and I am very interested in finding a job at a [movie theatre]. Because of your many years of experience as an executive with [Pacific Coast Cinemas], I would very much appreciate a chance to meet with you for career advice for someone like myself who is trying to find their first job. I know you are busy, but I only need twenty minutes out of your schedule. Would you have time to meet with me soon to discuss the aspects of your job? When would be a convenient date and time to come by the theatre to talk with you?

If you spoke over the phone, you'll need to send a very brief email to confirm the day and time of your meeting. Start your email by saying you appreciate their time and include your telephone number in the closing of your email to make it easy for the contact to get in touch with you. This should be sent no later than 24 hours after the meeting is confirmed.

SAMPLE EMAIL SCRIPT CONFIRMING YOUR MEETING

Dear [Ms. Jones],

Thank you for taking time out of your busy schedule to speak to me over the phone this afternoon. I am confirming our meeting on [April 10 at 1:00pm] at [the Pacific Coast Theatre in Redondo Beach].

I look forward to meeting with you.

Sincerely,

[George Michael

310 555 1234]

SAMPLE TELEPHONE SCRIPT CONFIRMING YOUR MEETING

Contact: This is [Ms. Jones].

You: Hello [Ms. Jones]. This is [George Michael]. I am calling to confirm our appointment at 1:00pm tomorrow.

Contact: Hello [George] Yes, we are confirmed for 1:00 tomorrow. Check in with the front desk when you arrive.

You: Thank you. I look forward to meeting with you.

Contact: Thank you. I'll see you tomorrow. Good bye.

You: Good bye.

TELEPHONE ETIQUETTE TIPS

When you call, remember:

- Practice what you are going to say so there are not a lot of 'ahhs', 'umm's' and pauses.

- Smile so it will come through in your voice.

- Use appropriate language.

- Do not talk to quickly, too slowly, too quietly, or too loudly.

- Do not chew gum, eat, smoke, or drink during your conversation.

- If you are leaving a message for a return call:

    o Make sure that the message on your voicemail message is professional and gives a favorable impression of who you are.

★

- ○ Make sure your voicemail isn't full and can receive messages.
- ○ If someone else is going to answer your phone, make sure they know that you are expecting a call and they are pleasant and polite when they speak with the caller.

TIPS FOR WRITING THANK YOU NOTES

Your note should be short and friendly. It can be a card that you mail or sent as an email. If you are mailing a card, choose one with a simple "Thank You" on the front on good quality notepaper with a matching envelope. This should go out no later than 24 hours after the meeting happened.

'THANK YOU' LETTER FORMAT

Date: Use the date the note is being sent.
Salutation: Address as Mr. or Ms. with the person's last name unless you knew them before the interview.
Paragraph 1: Thank the individual for taking the time to meet with you.
Paragraph 2: Share something you gained from your meeting.
Paragraph 3: Thank the individual again and express interest in working in his or her field or with their organization in the future.
Closing: Use "Sincerely," or "Yours Truly" and add your name.

SAMPLE 'THANK YOU' NOTE

April 10, 2017

Dear [Ms. Jones],

Thank you for taking the time to discuss your job as [Manager of the Pacific Coast Theatre] and talk about your organization. It was a pleasure meeting you and [getting a behind the scenes look at a movie theatre].

The information you shared provided me with a new perspective of the position, a better understanding of the requirements of the job, and an increased interest in finding a job [in any capacity with a movie theatre].

Again, thank you for your time. I appreciate the information you shared with me and I look forward to the possibility of one day becoming an associate [at a movie theatre just like yours].

Sincerely,

[George Michael]

NETWORKING AND LANDING A JOB: INFORMATIONAL INTERVIEW WORKSHEET

Person Interviewed: _____ **Date of Interview:** _____

Person's Title: _____ **Organization:** _____

Address: [insert rule] _____ **Phone Number:** _____

_____ **Email:** _____

QUESTIONS TO ASK AT THE INTERVIEW

Why did you choose to become a [_____]?

_____

_____

_____

What is a typical day like for you?

_____

_____

_____

What kind of skills would I need to be successful in this industry?

_____

_____

_____

What is a typical entry-level salary in this profession? How do the salaries progress in five years?

_____

_____

_____

What do you like most and least about your job?

_____

_____

_____

What preparation would you suggest for someone interested in entering this field?

_____

_____

_____

What do you wish you had known before you entered your career?

_____

_____

_____

Can you recommend anyone that I can contact about job opportunities in this industry?

_____

_____

_____

May I contact you in the future if I have any further questions? _____

_____

Remember, at the end of the meeting:

Thank the person for their time.

Ask for a business card.

★

QUESTIONS TO ASK YOURSELF AFTER THE INTERVIEW

1 Is this a career I would be interested in? *(circle one)*   YES   NO

If yes, why?

_____

_____

_____

If no, why not?

_____

_____

_____

2 What action can you take now to prepare yourself to achieve this goal?

Education: _____

Training: _____

Experience: _____

Community involvement: _____

Activities: _____

3 What action are you already taking to achieve your career goals in this field?

_____

_____

_____

4. What skills were mentioned in the interview that you already possess and can be added to your resume?

_____

_____

_____

NETWORKING AND LANDING A JOB: NETWORKING WORKSHEET

Referrals are the best source of job leads. Write down a list of people that you know and along with their job title.

Teacher/Subject

_____

_____

Counselors

_____

_____

Parents, Neighbors and Family Friends

_____

_____

Friends and Acquaintances

_____

_____

Volunteering is a good way to gain work experience and expand your network of professional contacts. List five issues that you are most passionate and organizations that are doing work in this area.

Issue	Organization
_____	_____
_____	_____
_____	_____
_____	_____
_____	_____

Internships provide excellent opportunities for entry-level jobs and ways to learn about the inner workings of the company. List five companies where you would like to work and the type of internship you would like.

Company	Type of Internship

Job fairs and Chamber of Commerce mixers are excellent places to connect to professionals in your field of interest and business owners with companies that have jobs in your field of interest. Do a Google search for upcoming job fairs in your area and check the website or your local Chamber of Commerce to find the dates, times, and locations for their upcoming events.

Job Fairs

Organizer of Fair	Date and Time	Location

Chamber of Commerce Mixers and Events

Event Name	Date and Time	Location

When attending a professional event, remember the following:

- Smile!
- Dress professionally matched to the culture of the companies at the event.
- When attending a job fair, bring at least 20 copies of your resume.
- When meeting recruiters, ask about job and career opportunities.
- Confidently recite :30 and :60 Elevator Pitch.
- Get a business card for everyone you meet; on the card, write down the date and the event where your meeting took place.
- At the end of a conversation, thank the person for their time.
- Write down important notes immediately after your meeting so you won't forget important details and information.
- Follow up all meetings with a thank you note or email.
- For recruiters, sent a short note every couple of weeks to check in and let them know that you are interested and available.

★

NETWORKING AND LANDING A JOB: SOCIAL MEDIA OVERVIEW

Your social media presence is not just a personal outlet. It is also your brand that identifies who you are, what you like to do, and the type of activities you like to participate in.

REASONS WHY YOU SHOULD HAVE A SOCIAL MEDIA PROFILE

- Employers regularly screen the social media sites of prospective job candidates and some see it as a red flag if the person has no social media presence.
- It's a good way to promote your skills, talents, and abilities.
- It's a good way to highlight honor roll awards and competition medals.
- It's a good way to connect to coworkers outside of the office.
- Many companies maintain a presence on many social media sites, so you should "like" the pages of any organizations where you'd like to work; checking these sites regularly is a good way to gather information about those organizations.

FOUNDATION OF A POSITIVE SOCIAL MEDIA PRESENCE

- Because what you post on social media represents you, make sure that all of the information on your profile is accurate and current.
- Do not post anything that could be viewed negatively by a future employer because it could impact your ability in being hired.
- Use the privacy settings to limit what other people can post on your profile and to prevent you from being tagged in other people's posts and pictures.
- Review the profiles of professionals you respect to see how they format their profile and what information they include.
- Make sure that your picture is recent, your hair was recently cut and is washed and combed. Men should be clean shaven.

RECOMMENDED PERSONAL SOCIAL MEDIA SITES

Facebook is one of the most popular social sites with over 1.79 billion active monthly users from around the world. When you become a friend with someone on Facebook, you both can view what they post and share articles, photos, and videos on each other's page. In the "About" link on your profile page, you can list your education and employment information. **Minimum age requirement: 13**

Twitter is a news and social networking service where users can post 140-character messages called "tweets". It has over 313 million active users and is popular with many celebrities, politicians, and social activists. In addition to posting tweets, you can "follow" other users to view their tweets. **Minimum age requirement: 13**

Pinterest is photo-sharing website where users can upload, save, sort, and manage images, known as "pins", which can be organized in folders sorted by a central topic or theme. When you have a Pinterest page, you can follow the pages and browse the contents of the pages of other users. If you are creative or have a special talent or skill, a Pinterest profile can be used as an online portfolio to display your artwork and projects. **Minimum age requirement: 13**

RECOMMENDED PROFESSIONAL SOCIAL MEDIA SITES

Monster and CareerBuilder are two of the most visited employment websites in the United States and around the world. Both sites allow users to search their job listings and company profiles and post online resumes. They also allow users to sign up for their online, career-advice newsletter and offer free services like resume critiques. **Minimum age requirement for both sites: 13**

LinkedIn is a business and employment-oriented social networking service with more than 467 million members including more than 40 million students and recent graduates in over 200 countries and territories. LinkedIn users can search their job listings, post a professional profile, and view information about potential employers. LinkedIn also allows users to post updates about their activities, share information, articles, and join "groups" that are focused on specific interests and topics. **Minimum age requirement: 18**

Indeed is a worldwide employment-related search engine of job listings that are aggregated from thousands of websites, job boards, staffing firms, associations, and company career pages. The site allows users to search their listings for available job openings and to post their resume online. **Minimum age requirement: 14, but adult supervision required for users under 18**

24 UNDERSTANDING THE WORKPLACE: WORKPLACE HIERARCHY CHART

Management Employees—Level 1
Chief Executive Officer
Chief Operating Officer
General Manager

Executive Employees—Level 2
President
Vice President
Executive Director
Chief Technical Officer
Chief Financial Officer
Community Relations Manager
Treasurer
Assistant Manager

Entry-Level Employees—Level 3
Administrative Assistant
Cashier
Sales Associate
Stock Clerk
Trainee
Intern

Non-Administrative Employees—Level 4
Security Guard
Custodian
Gardener
Foreman
Maintenance Worker

UNDERSTANDING THE WORKPLACE: LABOR LAW OVERVIEW

EMPLOYMENT CONTRACTS

Legally binding agreement between an employer and an employee regarding a term of employment. The agreement can be oral, written, or implied.

AT WILL EMPLOYMENT

An at-will employee can quit or be fired at any time for any reason that isn't illegal under state and federal laws. An employee cannot legally be fired for exercising their rights. If an employee is fired, it is up to the employer to show good cause for termination of the individual's employment.

INDEPENDENT CONTRACTORS

People who are self-employed in an independent trade, business, or profession in which they offer their services to the public are considered independent contractors. Independent contractors that earn more than $400 in a year must pay quarterly self-employment (SE) taxes based on their income. SE taxes are similar to the social security and Medicare taxes paid by employed workers.

EXEMPT VS NONEXEMPT

Nonexempt employees are typically paid an hourly wage, have a set work schedule, and are covered under all FLSA regulations like minimum wage laws and overtime regulations. *Exempt* employees are excluded from all FLSA rules. These are typically employees in executive, supervisory, professional, and outside sales jobs that draw a set salary and have a work schedule with varying hours.

FEDERAL INCOME TAX

Employers generally withhold federal income tax from an employee's wages. Upon being hired, a form W-4 is completed by the employee and this information is used to determine the amount of federal income tax that is withheld from each paycheck. Workers that make over $400 in a year must report their earnings to the Internal Revenue Service (commonly known as IRS) each year by April 15.

STATE INCOME TAX

In all but ten states (Alaska, Florida, Nevada, New Hampshire, South Dakota, Tennessee, Texas, Washington, and Wyoming), workers are required to pay an annual state income tax that is due on April 15 of each year.

SOCIAL SECURITY AND MEDICARE TAXES

Employers also deduct social security and Medicare taxes from each employee's paycheck.

FEDERAL LAWS

In the United States, the United States Department of Labor administers and enforces federal laws covering workplace activities for about 10 million employers and 125 million workers. These are listed below.

Wage and Hours

The Fair Labor Standards Act (FLSA) sets the standard for wages and is administered by the Wage and Hour Division (WHD) of the US Department of Labor. It establishes overtime pay of one-and-one-half times the regular rate of pay when an employee works over 40 hours in one week, but there are no overtime pay requirements for hours worked on weekends or holidays unless the employee has exceeded working 40 hours. The FLSA establishes 14 years of age as the minimum age for employment, limits the number of hours that children under the age of 16 can work, and forbids the employment of children under the age of 18 for jobs deemed too dangerous. The Wage and Hour Division also enforces the labor standard provisions of the immigration and Nationality Act that applies to aliens working in the under certain immigrant visa programs. The current federal minimum wage standard is $7.25.

Family and Medical Leave Act (FMLA)

Administered by the WHD, the FMLA requires employers of 50 or more employees to give up to 12 weeks of unpaid, job-protected leave to eligible employees for the birth or adoption of a child or for the serious illness of the employee or a spouse, child, or parent.

Workplace safety and health

The Occupational Safety and Health (OSH) Act is administered by the Occupational Safety and Health Administration (OSHA). It covers safety and health conditions for most private-sector and all public-sector employees to guarantee employees are free from being exposed to recognized, serious hazards in the workplace.

Whistleblower and retaliation protections

OSHA administers the "whistleblower" protection provisions of twenty-two states. Under this law, an employee may file a complaint with OSHA if they believe that they have received discrimination or retaliation for exercising any right afforded by OSH. An employee must file a complaint about any health or safety issues within 30 days after the occurrence of the alleged violation.

Worker Adjustment and Retraining Notification Act

This federal law mandates that workers being laid off be given a written 60 days' notice before the date of mass layoffs or plant closings. A worker that does not receive notice per the law may seek damages for back pay and benefits for up to 60 days depending on how many days of notice they received.

Harassment

Harassment in the workplace based on race, color, religion, sex, national origin, age, and disability in any form is prohibited by federal law. It becomes unlawful when the offensive conduct becomes a condition of continued employment or the conduct is severe or pervasive enough to create a work environment that a reasonable person would consider intimidating, hostile, or abusive. An employer is automatically held liable for harassment by a supervisor that results in a negative employment action such as termination, failure to promote, or be hired. An employer is also held liable if it was known or should have been known about the harassment and they failed to take prompt and appropriate corrective action. The Equal Employment Opportunity Commission (EEOC) handles administration and enforcement of laws covering harassment.

Sexual harassment

Sexual harassment includes unwelcome sexual advances, requests for sexual favors, remarks about a person's sex, and other verbal or physical harassment of a sexual nature. The victim or abuser can be either a male or female and can be the victim's supervisor, supervisor in another area, a coworker, or non-employee.

STATE LAWS

State regulations vary from state to state and the regulations for the state where you work. Below are the laws as they apply in the state of California:

State minimum wage rates

If the state rate is higher than the federal rate, the state rate would apply. In California, the minimum wage is $10.00 for employers with less than 25 employees and $10.50 for employers with 26 or more employees.

Minimum rest periods

A paid ten-minute rest period is required for every four hours worked. This does not apply for employees that work less than three and a half hours in a day.

Minimum meal periods

An employee is entitled to an unpaid half-hour meal period after five hours of work. If an employee works six hours or fewer, an employer and employee may consent to waive the meal period. For a work day of over ten hours, an employee is entitled to a second meal period of no fewer than 30 minutes.

Payday requirements

The minimum that an employee must be paid is at least twice during each calendar month, but there are variations on this law per the occupation. Some occupations that are excluded include executive, administrative, farm, and labor contract workers, or an employee of a motor vehicle dealer that is paid on commission.

State unemployment insurance benefits

The Federal-State Unemployment Insurance Program provides temporary financial benefits to unemployed workers. Each state administers their own program within guidelines established by federal law. Benefit amounts are based on a percentage of an individual's earnings over a recent 52-week period up to a maximum amount established by the state for up to 26 weeks. The funding for the program in most states is provided by a tax imposed on employers. Benefits paid to recipients must be reported on a federal income tax return.

Worker's compensation

Workers' compensation (also known as workmans' comp) is a state-mandated insurance program that provides financial benefits to employees who suffer job-related injuries and illnesses. The federal government administers the program which provides replacement benefits, medical treatment, vocational rehabilitation, and other benefits, but each state establishes the rules and regulations for the workmans' comp program in their state. In general, an employee with a work-related illness or injury can get workmans' comp benefits regardless of who was at fault. In exchange for these guaranteed benefits, employees usually do not have the right to sue their employer in court for damages they've incurred due to their injuries.

FILING A GRIEVANCE

- Wage and Hour Division: www.dol.gov/wecanhelp/howtofile complaint.htm

- Family and Medical Leave Act: Call 866 487 9243

- OSHA: www.osha.gov/workers/file_complaint.html or call 800 321 6742

UNDERSTANDING THE WORKPLACE: AMERICANS WITH DISABILITIES ACT (ADA) OVERVIEW

WHAT IS THE AMERICANS WITH DISABILITIES ACT (ADA)?

- Civil rights law that prohibits discrimination against individuals with disabilities in all areas of public life

- Purpose is to make sure that people with disabilities have the same rights and opportunities as everyone else

- Signed into law by president George W. Bush in 1990

- Divided into five titles (or sections) that relate to different areas of public life

    o Title I: Employment—we will only be discussing this

    o Title II: State and Local Government

    o Title III: Public Accommodations

    o Title IV: Telecommunications

    o Title V: Miscellaneous Provisions

TITLE I: EMPLOYMENT

- Designed to help people with disabilities access the same employment opportunities and benefits that are available to people without disabilities

- Applies to employers with 15 or more employees

- Requires employers to provide *reasonable accommodations* to qualified employees and applicants

- *Reasonable accommodations* are changes in the workplace that accommodate employees with disabilities without causing the employer "undue hardship, too great a difficulty or expense"

- Regulated and enforced by the US Equal Employment Opportunity Commission (EEOC)

- Enforced by the US Department of Justice

WHAT IS A DISABILITY UNDER THE ADA?

- Individual with a disability is someone who has:

  º Physical or mental impairment that substantially limits one or more major life activities

  º Must have documentation of a disability or impairment

  º No complete list of disabilities covered by the ADA, but EEOC published documents that would easily be considered a disability within the meaning of the law. These include:

    – autism

    – intellectual disabilities

    – medical conditions: diabetes, cancer

    – mobility impairments requiring the use of a wheelchair

    – post-traumatic stress disorder

    – cerebral palsy

    – multiple sclerosis

HOW DOES THE ADA AFFECT INDIVIDUALS IN THE WORKPLACE?

- Employers are required to provide reasonable accommodations for a job, work environment, or the way things are done so individuals with disabilities can enjoy equal access to the workplace and enjoy the same benefits that are available to non-disabled individuals.

- "Reasonable accommodations" must be tailored to the needs of the individual and the requirements of the job.

- Accommodations must be agreed to between the employer and the employee.

QUESTIONS TO CONSIDER WHEN DECIDING ON ACCOMMODATIONS FOR AN INDIVIDUAL WITH AUTISM

- What limitations does the employee with ASD experience?
- How do these limitations affect the employee's job performance?
- What specific job tasks are a problem as a result of these limitations?
- What accommodations are available to reduce or eliminate these problems?
- Are all possible resources being used to determine the accommodations?
- Can the employee with ASD provide information on possible accommodation solutions?
- Do supervisory personnel and employees need training regarding ASD?
- Once accommodations are in place, would it be useful to meet with the employee to evaluate the effectiveness of the accommodations and to determine whether additional or alternative accommodations are needed?

SAMPLE OF SUPPORTS THAT WOULD BE CONSIDERED REASONABLE ACCOMMODATIONS FOR MOST EMPLOYERS

Supports to assist with speaking and communicating

- Allow an employee to provide written responses instead of verbal responses
- Allow an employee to bring an advocate to a performance review or disciplinary meeting

Executive functioning/time management supports

- Divide large assignments into smaller tasks
- Use a wall calendar to help emphasize dates
- Develop a color-code system to organize files, projects, or activities

★

- Use a job coach to teach/reinforce organization skills
- Provide a "cheat sheet" of high-priority activities, projects, and people
- Provide written instructions for tasks
- Help an employee remember the faces of coworkers by providing a directory with pictures and providing coworkers with name tags
- Provide written instructions of tasks and projects
- Allow additional training time for learning new tasks

Supports in working with supervisors

- Allow a supervisor to prioritize tasks
- Provide a work buddy to help the "learn the ropes"
- Provide weekly or monthly meetings to reflect on the employee's performance, discuss any workplace issues, and target any areas that need improvement
- When there is a change in the employee's supervisor, allow old and new supervisor to keep open their channels of communication to support the employee during the transition

Sensory supports

- Allow an employee to use a hand-held squeeze ball
- Provide noise-cancelling headphones to reduce noise to help the employee focus
- Relocate an employee's office away from audible or visual distractions
- Change out fluorescent interior lighting
- Allow telecommuting when possible

Stress management

- Allow an employee to make telephone calls for support
- Modify employee's work schedule

On-the-job social skills supports

- Provide a job coach to help understand social cues
- Help employee "learn the ropes" by providing a mentor
- Use training videos to demonstrate appropriate social cues
- Make attendance at social functions optional

How do you negotiate for a reasonable accommodation?

- An employee is responsible for informing or disclosing their disability to their employer and can request reasonable accommodations that they need to do their job.
- An employer and employee must engage in what the law calls a "flexible interactive process" to discuss and agree accommodations that are effective and practical.

What is an undue hardship exception?

- The ADA does not require employers to make accommodations that would be considered an undue hardship or any changes that would impose a significant cost or impact upon the business.

Am I required to disclose that I have a disability?

- No, an employee is *not* required to disclose disability to their employee.
- To benefit from the protections provided under the ADA, the employee must disclose their disability. If there is no disclosure, there are no ADA protections.

How should I disclose my disability?

- Disclose disability on a "need-to-know" basis
- Provide details about disability as it applies to your work-related accommodations
- Disclose to an individual who has authority to grant request
- Supervisor needs to be informed of your disability-related needs so they can provide the necessary supports and judge your job performance fairly.

Can an employer discriminate against an employee because of a disability?

- No. The ADA forbids discrimination when it comes to any aspect of employment, including:

  ○ hiring

  ○ firing

  ○ promotions

  ○ layoffs

  ○ pay or wages

  ○ job assignments

  ○ benefits

  ○ training

What questions can and can't an employer ask in regards to an employee's disability?

- How the employee can perform the job, with or without a reasonable accommodation

- An employer can't ask a job applicant to answer medical questions or take a medical exam before extending a job offer.

- An employer can't ask if an applicant has a disability.

- After being hired, an employer can only ask medical questions or require a medical exam for documentation to support an employee's request of accommodations.

★

UNDERSTANDING THE WORKPLACE: CONFLICT RESOLUTION STRATEGIES

THOMAS-KILMANN (TKI) STRATEGY

Accommodate
This strategy is a form of 'giving in' and letting the other person inthe conflict have their way.

Pros: It quickly resolves the conflict.

Cons: The person that is doing the accommodating may become resentful.

Avoid
This strategy postpones resolving the conflict indefinitely.

Pros: Time may help the conflict may resolve itself.

Cons: The conflict and bad feelings may increase the longer the conflict is left unresolved.

Collaborate
This strategy requires integrating multiple ideas to help resolve a conflict.

Pros: If effectively used, a solution will be reached that is acceptable to everyone.

Cons: It takes time and may be difficult to get all parties to agree.

Compromise
This strategy requires all parties to give up something in order to find a solution that is acceptable to all parties.

Pros: Once reached, the solution will seem fair to all parties.

Cons: It takes time and may be difficult to get each person to give up something.

Compete
This strategy pits coworkers against one another and has a definite winner and loser in the resolution of the conflict.

Pros: This works best in an emergency or crisis situation when time is of the essence in finding a solution.

Cons: It puts people against one another, and the loser will probably harbor resentment.

★

UNDERSTANDING THE WORKPLACE: CONFLICT RESOLUTION STRATEGIES

INTEREST-BASED RELATIONAL (IBR) APPROACH

Ground rules

Encourage people to:

- ☐ listen with empathy and see the conflict from each other's point of view

- ☐ explain issues clearly and concisely

- ☐ use "I" rather than "you" statements so no one feels attacked

- ☐ be clear about their feelings

- ☐ remain flexible and adaptable

Technique

Step 1. Make sure good relationships are a priority

Treat others with respect and acknowledge their viewpoint even if you don't agree. Be mindful during your discussion—stay calm, exercise acceptance, and be patient.

Step 2. Separate people from problems

Separate the issue from the person. Put personal feelings aside and address only the issue that is causing the conflict.

Step 3. Listen carefully to different interests

Keep the conversation courteous and don't blame the other person. Ask for the other person's perspective to identify the issue that the person thinks is causing the conflict.

Step 4. Listen first, talk second

Listen to other people's points of view without defending your own. Make sure that each person has finished talking before speaking. Identify what the person thinks is the issue and ask questions if you need clarification.

★

Step 5. Determine out the facts

Be fair and balanced in the gathering of information. Acknowledge the other person's feelings. Make sure the person feels listened to and has been a part of the discussion.

Step 6. Explore options together

By this point, the conflict may have already been resolved once everyone's views have been heard and understood, but it's important to be open to an alternate position. If needed, brainstorm ideas and be open to all suggestions to come to an agreement that will result in a satisfying outcome.

UNDERSTANDING THE WORKPLACE: AWN RULES FOR DATING COWORKERS

DON'T DATE YOUR BOSS

Most employers have a policy that prohibits direct supervisors from dating their subordinates, and this is for good reason. If the relationship ends badly, a disgruntled employee could claim a hostile work environment and sue the company for harassment. A manager–subordinate romance can also create a perception of favoritism, which can lead to tension among coworkers that report to the same manager.

YOU CAN ONLY ASK YOUR COWORKER OUT ONE TIME

If you want to ask out a coworker, you only have one chance. If you continually ask out a coworker after being told no the first time, the coworker could claim a hostile working environment and report the incident to HR. The consequence of these actions might get you a bad reputation at work or, if the incident is serious, result in you being fired from your job.

AVOID PUBLIC DISPLAYS OF AFFECTION (PDAS)

If you are dating someone at work, it isn't considered professional to kiss or hug in front of your colleagues. These actions can make other people uncomfortable or possibly make others jealous.

DISCLOSE TO YOUR COMPANY

It's best to disclose to your supervisor when you start dating a coworker. Letting your boss know about your relationship will keep you out of the workplace rumor mill and avoid the awkward situation when everyone at work finds out that you're a couple.

SET BOUNDARIES

Spending all your time with a boyfriend and girlfriend might not be good for your relationship. If you ever starting dating a coworker, it's ok to schedule time for by yourself and with other friends to share in the hobbies and activities that you enjoy most.

PLAN FOR THE ENDING

Relationships do end, which can be a problem if you were seeing someone that you also see every day at work. This could seriously impact your job, especially if the relationship ends very badly. Before you ask out a coworker, just remember that you're mixing business with pleasure. If the relationship works out, that's great, but if it doesn't, it could create a bad situation at work that might be impossible to fix.

AUTISM WORKS NOW Recall and Review

25 WORKSHOP REVIEW

Name: _____

Date: _____

Name three things we did in the Roundtable Discussion.

1. _____
2. _____
3. _____

Name three things we did in Prepare and Practice.

1. _____
2. _____
3. _____

What were some upcoming events that we discussed?

1. _____
2. _____
3. _____

What do you need to do before the next workshop?

1. _____
2. _____
3. _____

List at least one thing you learned or know about someone else.

Candidate name	Other person	What you learned

26 WORKSHOP QUIZ

Name: _____

Date: _____

WORKSHOP QUIZ 10/6/16

True or False: Everything I'll be learning in the workshop will help me get and keep a job.

- ☐ True
- ☐ False

On the 5-Point Scale, I'm calm when I'm at a level:

- ☐ 5
- ☐ 1
- ☐ 3

An interview should take approximately:

- ☐ 15 minutes
- ☐ 1 hour
- ☐ 2 hours

How early should I get to an appointment?

- ☐ I should arrive at the exact time I need to be at my appointment.
- ☐ 15 minutes
- ☐ 1 hour

What can I do when I start feeling stressed?

- ☐ Mindful breathing
- ☐ Close my eyes and count to 10
- ☐ Stretch my body
- ☐ All of the above

238

AUTISM WORKS NOW Field Trips and Guest Speakers

27 WORKSHOP SESSION REVIEW: WORKPLACE HABITS AND EXPECTATIONS

WORKPLACE HABITS AND EXPECTATIONS
Courtesy of the Miller Career and Transition Center in Reseda, California

- Work is not what you see on television; work is not like school. Work is not like home; work is like…well work!

- Focus on greatness and believe in yourself. You can do it!

- Have a positive attitude—nothing is more important. You are in charge of your attitude! Be friendly, kind, courteous and customer service oriented!

- Take initiative, stay focused, stay busy, and be responsible for your work.

- Follow the lead and instructions given to you by your supervisor.

- Follow all equipment and workplace safety guidelines.

- Dress appropriately in clean clothes without holes, rips, or stains.

- Use proper hygiene: wash and comb your hair, clean your nails, shower, and apply deodorant. Men should shave daily.

- Remember, you're at work and not on a date so act appropriately.

- Work is work and not social time. Break time is for social time.

- Interact productively with you coworkers in a positive manner. You're a team player!

- Demonstrate respect to your coworkers and supervisors.

- Take constructive criticism in a professional manner.

- Advocate for yourself. If you don't know or are unsure, ask questions.

★

28 WORKSHOP SESSION REVIEW: WORKSHOP SYLLABUS

MISSION OF THE WORKPLACE READINESS WORKSHOP

To help individuals on the autism spectrum acquire the skills they need to get and keep a job.

OUR BELIEFS

1. Individuals on the autism spectrum and with related learning differences can develop essential employment skills.

2. Individuals with autism deserve meaningful jobs that contribute to the well-being of their communities and provide a living wage.

3. Employers will be motivated to hire individuals with autism when they experience first-hand the positive contributions that these individuals contribute to the workplace.

INSTRUCTORS AND CONTACT INFORMATION

First name, last name _____

Phone # _____

Email address _____

Workshop address _____

Workshop dates _____

Workshop times _____

CANDIDATE REQUIREMENTS

- **Candidates must have the ability to independently operate a computer.** If they need individualized computer support in order to participate in class, it is their responsibility to make arrangements to provide their own classroom aide.

- **Candidates are expected to complete assigned homework by the due date.** Work assigned outside of class is designed to reinforce the concepts that are presented in class. To get as much out of the workshop as possible candidates should complete all assignments by the due date.

MISSED SESSIONS

There is no refund for missed sessions. Upon request, candidates will be given access to or copies of the materials that were distributed in class.

WORKSHOP SESSION REVIEW: WORKSHOP EXPECTATIONS

In order for our community to operate smoothly and conflict-free, the following are the expected behaviors of candidates participating in any AWN class and activity.

Every member of our community deserves respect. All members are expected to be respectful at all times towards all others in their words, thoughts, and actions at all times. No exceptions!

Candidates are expected to arrive on time and ready to learn.

Community members will be *asked to leave the class* if they:

- break the "respect everyone at all times" rule
- behave in a way that disrupts class

Candidates may be allowed to return to class if they can calm themselves down and apologize for their behavior.

Looking at your phone or surfing the web during class instruction is not being mindful. *Cell phones are to be turned off and put away and computers may be used for instructional purposes only.* A candidate that chooses not to follow this rule may be asked to leave the class.

Conversations and questions unrelated to classroom discussions are permitted during breaks, before, and after class. Candidates that engage in off topic conversations during class discussions will be directed back to the topic of the classroom conversation.

Outside food may not be eaten in class. Any candidate that brings food to class will be asked to leave the class and return after they have finished eating.

Everything you are learning in the workshop will help you reach your goal of getting and keeping a job. *Have fun and enjoy yourselves!*

29 FIELD TRIP RECAP—SAMPLE

BEST BUY FIELD TRIP RECAP 11/10/16
With Manager, Brian Wilson

What are the various jobs at Best Buy?
- Seasonal Cashier: this is how Brian started at Best Buy
- Customer Assistance: checking receipts, checking on safety
- Inventory: online and receiving merchandise from trucks
- Merchandising: creating look and feel of store
- Sales Associates
- Administrative: accounting
- Geek Squad

What are the traits that successful employees of Best Buy have in common?
- They enjoy what they do.
- They have passion for serving customers.
- They find satisfaction in solving problems.
- They strive to meet the expectations of customers.
- Advice: Customers are allowed to have a bad day. Employees aren't.

If I were going to apply for a job at Best Buy, what advice would you give me?
- Make sure that working at Best Buy is something you would enjoy.
- Don't be motivated to take a job for the paycheck.
- Money is a necessity but be motivated to work doing something you like.

★

What is a typical day like at Best Buy?

- Each day is different, but the goal for associates is to ask questions of customers to help them find what is needed:
  - ○ What brings you into Best Buy?
  - ○ Are you replacing an item or is this the first time buying?
  - ○ If you are replacing, how long since you last replaced?
  - ○ What will you use it for?

What types of jobs did you have before you worked at Best Buy?

- Best Buy was his first job and he has worked there for eight years.
- Started at 17 as a seasonal cashier. Wanted to be a lawyer, so left to go to school. Returned when he finished school. He's been back for five years.
- Plans to return to school to finish his law degree.

Do you offer full and part time jobs at Best Buy?

- Yes. Also, seasonal and year-round.

Do you receive company discounts?

- Yes, and vendors also give employees discounts, sometimes better than store. Reason is to have the employees use the merchandise then promote it to customers.

Instructor materials

- Assessments
  - Work Smarts Group Spreadsheet
  - Interest Inventory Spreadsheet
- Roundtable Discussion
  - Icebreaker Questions
  - Inspirational Quotes
- Prepare and Practice
  - Dress for Success Presentation Template: Can I Wear This To Work?
  - Conflict Resolution Role-Playing Scenarios
- Field Trips
  - Sample Questions for candidates

Assessments

WORK SMARTS GROUP SPREADSHEET

After candidates complete their Work Smarts assessment, the results are tallied, color coded, and compiled on a Google Sheet. The spreadsheet is then shared with the group so everyone can see who has similar learning style and interests. It is also projected on screen during class so the group can view it together. The following is an example spreadsheet.

Cathy	Clark	Lucy	Parker	Steven	Wyatt
Music / 27	People / 25	Word / 27	Body / 30	Picture / 27	Body / 29
People / 24	Nature / 24	Body / 26	People / 30	Self / 24	Nature / 24
Body / 23	Picture / 24	People / 26	Music / 29	Body / 22	Picture / 24
Self / 22	Logic / 21	Picture / 26	Word / 29	Music / 22	Music / 21
Picture / 21	Self / 21	Nature / 26	Nature / 29	Word / 20	People / 21
Word / 20	Body/ 20	Music / 22	Logic / 28	Logic / 19	Self / 20
Logic / 19	Music / 20	Self / 23	Picture / 28	People / 19	Logic / 16
Nature / 19	Word / 19	Logic / 21	Self / 26	Nature / 16	Word / 14

Assessments

INTERESTS INVENTORY SPREADSHEET

After candidates complete the Interests Inventory, the results are tallied and similar interests are color coded. The information is compiled on a Google Sheet and this is shared with the group to help candidates identify what interests they share with other members of the group. It is also projected on screen during class so the group can view it together. The following is an example spreadsheet.

	Cathy	**Clark**	**Lucy**	**Parker**	**Steven**	**Wyatt**
Do in free time	Talk to friends Browse Web Take a walk	Music	Gaming Be with pets	Computer Movies Shop	Art Computer Write	Computer Music Cook
Favorite school subject	Art History Science	Art	Art Science History	Art Choir English	Band PE History	Math Language Arts
Favorite books	Manga Animals Fiction	Animals	Photography Architecture Travel	Hunger Games Harry Potter	Fairy tales Disney	Disney Cooking Travel
Sports, hobbies	Drawing Cooking	Animals	Hiking Photography Painting	Collecting Soccer Running	Swimming Soccer Track and field	Soccer Baseball Swimming
Internet	YouTube	YouTube	YouTube Google	YouTube Facebook	YouTube	YouTube Google
Do for long time	Movies Television	Travel Games	Computer Read	Movies Music	Disney Movies	Swim Run

Roundtable Discussion

ICEBREAKER QUESTIONS

Icebreaker questions are used to help candidates get to know one another better and to help them learn information about members of the group. The best icebreaker topics are ones that are appropriate to discuss at work. The following is just a partial list so add new questions that are appropriate for your group.

What pets do you have or would you like to have?

What is your favorite vacation and why?

What is your favorite type of food and favorite restaurant?

Describe the best meal you ever ate.

Is there any person living or dead that you would like to meet?

Name three items that you would take with you if your house was burning down.

What skill would you like to learn?

If money was no object, what would you buy?

If you had $10,000, what would you spend it on?

If you could be granted a superpower, what would it be?

What is your favorite movie?

What is your favorite TV show?

If you could choose an imaginary friend, who would you choose and why?

If you were stranded on a desert island, what three things would you want to have with you?

What is your favorite cartoon and why?

If you had your own talk show, who would be your first three guests?

Roundtable Discussion

INSPIRATIONAL QUOTES

Inspirational quotes are read at the beginning of class and how the statement applies to work is discussed. The goal is to convey important workplace information in short, easy statements so candidates can remember what they've learned after they finish the workshop. There are a limitless number of inspirational quotes that are easy to find in a Google search. It's best to use a quote that relates to the topic being covered in Prepare and Practice.

CONNECTING TO COWORKERS

"I've learned that people will forget what you said, people will forget what you did, but people will never forget how you made them feel." Maya Angelou

How this is connected to work: Your coworkers will like you more if you have a positive attitude and are respectful at all times.

"Great minds discuss ideas; average minds discuss events; small minds discuss people." Eleanor Roosevelt

How this relates to work: You'll want to be the average range when speaking to coworkers. Not everyone has a great mind like yours and coworkers won't always be as interested in your special interests as you are. Small minds gossip and talk about others when they aren't there and this isn't appreciated or respected by others.

INTERVIEW ESSENTIALS: PERSEVERANCE

"If you're trying to achieve, there will be roadblocks. I've had them; everybody has had them. But obstacles don't have to stop you. If you run into a wall, don't turn around and give up. Figure out how to climb it, go through it, or work around it." Michael Jordan

How this relates to work: Don't give up—it takes a lot of time and effort to find a job.

"I've missed more than 9000 shots in my career. I've lost almost 300 games. 26 times, I've been trusted to take the game-winning shot and missed. I've failed over and over and over again in my life. And that is why I succeed." Michael Jordan

How this relates to work: Don't give up—it takes a lot of time and effort to find a job.

"There are no mistakes in life. There are only learning opportunities." Susan Osborne

How this relates to work: If you make a mistake at work, don't be upset, learn from it.

LANDING A JOB: PREPARATION

"Success occurs when opportunity meets preparation." Zig Zigler

How this relates to work: In order to get a job, you need to prepare.

LANDING A JOB: STARTING A NEW JOB

"You can learn new things at any time in your life if you're willing to be a beginner. If you actually learn to like being a beginner, the whole world opens up to you." Barbara Sher

How this relates to work: You will need to be in your job for some time before you are good at it.

DRESS FOR SUCCESS PRESENTATION TEMPLATE: CAN I WEAR THIS TO WORK?

The attached presentation template was created on Google Slides and includes placeholders where pictures can be inserted. A Google search using "Images" is an easy way to locate pictures that can be used in your presentation. Under the Fair Use rule, you do not need to ask permission from an author or copyright holder when using copyrighted materials for educational purposes.

The month you are covering Dress for Success, add slides with men's and women's attire that matches the culture of the company you'll be visiting for your field trip. For example, if the month you'll be using the presentation you're scheduled to visit a pet supply store, the men's and women's slide should include people wearing polo shirts and khaki pants.

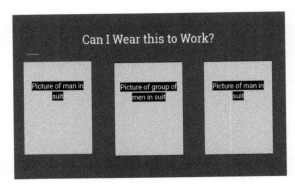

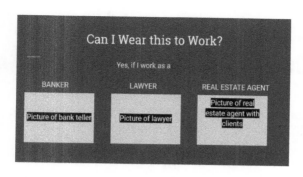

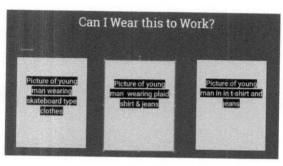

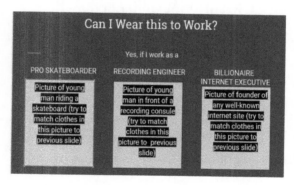

ALWAYS REMEMBER ...

Wear clothes that fit properly - know your measurements.

Wear clothes to the job that match the workplace.

Dressing for success is dressing for the job that you want.

Keep your professional wardrobe clean and in good repair.

Prepare and Practice

CONFLICT RESOLUTION ROLE-PLAYING SCENARIOS

The goal of the exercise will be to have candidates practice both the TKI and IBR conflict resolution strategies.

TKI STRATEGY

Avoid

Accommodate

Complete

Compromise

Collaborate

INTEREST-BASED RELATIONAL (IBR) APPROACH

Step 1. Make sure good relationships are a priority

Step 2. Separate people from problems

Step 3. Listen carefully to different viewpoints

Step 4. Listen first, talk second

Step 5. Determine the facts

Step 6. Explore options together

HOW TO FACILITATE THE ACTIVITY

Read through a scenario and discuss the options using both techniques.

TKI: Discuss the pros and cons of each strategy
Choose the strategy that would end the conflict

ABI: Discuss how each step can be implemented
Decide on the best solution to end the conflict

★

SCENARIOS

Below are some scenarios that can be used in conflict resolution role-playing activities using the TKI and IBR conflict resolution techniques. You can also create your own scenarios. Ask candidates for suggestions. If they feel comfortable, encourage them to share a conflict they experienced in their own life and use it as one of the scenarios. All of the scenarios included are related to work, but for a class of middle and high school students, they will most likely have very little experience as an employee. These students will find the activity more meaningful if it is related to a conflict they experienced at school, at home, or out in the community.

Scenario 1

You are working in an upscale music store. One of your coworkers makes fun of your clothes all the time. The coworker is not a very good dresser and you could easily make fun of the way the coworker dresses.

Scenario 2

Your coworker listens to music on his computer with headphones on. However, he often ends up going to sleep and snoring loudly, which irritates his coworkers.

Scenario 3

You work in an office and share a cubicle with Sally, who likes to talk a lot about politics. You do not share her opinions and find her political views to be extreme. You like Sally and want to get along with her, but her political beliefs are so far away from yours that you are starting to have a hard time stopping yourself from saying anything that opposes Sally's beliefs.

Scenario 4

You're waiting for a ride outside of work when you observe two of the company security workers loading boxes of paper into a van and driving off. You've seen this happen more than once and suspect the guards may be stealing. They are quite large and tough looking.

Scenario 5

You are the secretary for a large bank, and the bank manager is in a meeting. You have been instructed to take messages for all of the manager's calls and tell the callers that he will return their call when he is out of his meeting. A customer calls and demands to talk with the bank manager, but you do as you are told and ask to take a message. The man gets angry and starts using abusive language towards you.

Scenario 6

You share an office with two other coworkers. One coworker, Jamal, likes to talk a lot about his family and personal life. Your other coworker, Blake, used to listen politely, but he is becoming increasingly annoyed every time Jamal starts to discuss his personal life. You find Jamal's monologues amusing, but you are also aware that Blake is slowly getting angrier and angrier. Jamal is also getting irritated with Blake. When he talks, he notices that Blake stares at the computer in an attempt to tune him out, and Jamal thinks this is very rude. You are sure that sooner or later your coworkers are going to have a major fight. You get along very well with both of our coworkers, but you don't want to get into the middle of anything.

Field Trips

SAMPLE QUESTIONS FOR CANDIDATES

The following are examples of questions that can be assigned to candidates for use during the question and answer portion of the field trip. Each question should be personalized with the name of the company or industry that you are visiting. Feel free to add to the list with questions that you've created based on your own research.

How did you get started in this industry?

What inspired you to work in your industry?

What do you like most about working at your company?

What jobs did you have before working at your company?

What is the culture of your company?

What are the various jobs and departments at your company?

What traits in common do successful employees at your organization have?

What is a typical day like at your company?

What accomplishment are you most proud of?

What do you see for the future of your company?

If I wanted to work at your company, what type of work experience would be beneficial?

Which companies are your biggest competitors?

References

Alfano, C.A., Beidel, D.C., and Turner, S.M. (2006). "Cognitive correlates of social phobia among children and adolescents." *Journal of Abnormal Child Psychology, 34*, 2, 182–194.

American RadioWorks (2014). The troubled history of vocational education. Retrieved on March 8, 2017 from www.americasjobexchange.com/career-advice/how-to-make-a-good-first-impression-at-work

Americas Job Exchange (2017). *Starting a New Job—How to Make a Good First Impression.* Retrieved on March 8, 2017 from www.americasjobexchange.com/career-advice/how-to-make-a-good-first-impression-at-work

Autism Speaks (2016). *Frequently Asked Questions.* Retrieved on March 8, 2016 from www.autismspeaks.org/what-autism/faq?gclid=CjOKEQjwuJu9BRDP

Bar, M., Neta, M., and Linz, H. (2006). "Very first impressions." *Emotion, 6*, 269–278.

Baron-Cohen, S. (1997). *Mindblindness: An Essay on Autism and Theory of Mind.* Cambridge, MA: MIT Press.

Billstedt, E., Gillberg, C., and Gillberg, C. (2005). "Autism after adolescence: population-based 13- to 22-year follow-up study of 120 individuals with autism diagnosed in childhood." *Journal of Autism and Developmental Disorders, 35*, 3, 351–360.

Biswal, R. (2016). "Top 16 Most Popular Google Products and Services." Retrieved on March 8, 2017, from www.ecloudbuzz.com/most-popular-google-products-services

Blair, I.V., Judd, C.M., and Chapleau, K.M. (2004). "The influence of Afrocentric facial features in criminal sentencing." *Psychological Science, 15*, 674–679.

Bock, M.A. (2001). "SODA Strategy: Enhancing the social interaction skills of youngsters with Asperger Syndrome." *Intervention in School and Clinic, 36*, 272–278.

Brown, F., McDonnell, J., and Snell, M.E. (2016). *Instruction of Students with Severe Disabilities (8th edn).* Boston, MA: Pearson.

Brown, M., Setren, E., and Topa, G. (2016) "Do Informal Referrals Lead to Better Matches? Evidence from a Firm's Employee Referral System." *Journal of Labor Economics 34*, 1, 161–209.

Buron, K.D., and Curtis, M. (2003). *The Incredible 5-Point Scale: Assisting Students with Autism Spectrum Disorders in Understanding Social Interactions and Controlling their Emotional Responses.* Shawnee Mission, KS: Autism Asperger Publishing Company.

CareerBuilder (2014). Number of Employers Passing on Applicants Due to Social Media Posts Continues to Rise, According to New CareerBuilder Survey. Retrieved on March 8, 2017 from www.careerbuilder.com/share/aboutus/pressreleasesdetail.aspx?sd=6%2F26%2F2014&id=pr829&ed=12%2F31%2F2014

Cohn, A. (2001). *Positive behavioral supports: Information for educators.* Retrieved April 20, 2017 from www.naspcenter.org/factsheets/pbs_fs.html

Devine, G. (2015) 10 Reasons to Dress for Success. Retrieved on March 8, 2017 from www.linkedin.com/pulse/10-reasons-dress-success-gerard-devine

Durand, V.M., and Crimmins, D.B. (1992). *The Motivation Assessment Scale (MAS) Administration Guide.* Monaco and Associates.

Durand, V. M., and Merges, E. (2001). Functional communication training a contemporary behavior analytic intervention for problem behaviors. *Focus on Autism and Other Developmental Disabilities, 16*, 2, 110–119.

Eberhardt, J.L., Davies, P.G., Purdie-Vaughns, V.J., and Johnson, S.L. (2006). "Looking deathworthy: Perceived stereotypicality of Black defendants predicts capital-sentencing outcomes." *Psychological Science, 17*, 383–386.

Fisher, R., Ury, W.L., and Patton, B. (2011). *Getting to Yes: Negotiating Agreement Without Giving In.* New York: Penguin.

Gardner, H. (1991). *The Unschooled Mind: How Children Think and How Schools Should Teach.* New York: Basic Books.

Guerin, L. (2017a). *Employment At Will: What Does it Mean?* Retrieved on March 8, 2017 from www.nolo.com/legal-encyclopedia/employment-at-will-definition-30022.html

Guerin, L. (2017b). *Types of Employment Contracts.* Retrieved on March 8, 2017 from www.nolo.com/legal-encyclopedia/types-employment-contracts.html

HG.org (2017). *What is Employment Law?* Retrieved on March 8, 2017 from www.hg.org/employ.html

Hierarchy Structure (2011). *Company Employee Hierarchy.* Retrieved on March 8, 2017 from www.hierarchystructure.com/company-employee-hierarchy/

House, J.S., Landis, K.R., and Umberson, D. (1988). "Social relationships and health." *Science, 241*, 4865, 540–545.

Individuals with Disability Education Act Amendments of 1997 [IDEA]. Retrieved June 4, 2017 from https://www2.ed.gov/about/offices/list/oii/nonpublic/idea1.html

Ingram, D. (2016) *Why is Organizational Structure Important?* Retrieved on March 8, 2017 from http://smallbusiness.chron.com/organizational-structure-important-3793.html

Kahneman, D., and Deaton, A. (2010). High income improves evaluation of life but not emotional well-being. Proceedings of the national academy of sciences, 107(38), 16489–16493.

Kilmann, R.H., and Thomas, K.W. (1975). "Interpersonal conflict-handling behavior as reflections of Jungian personality dimensions." *Psychological Reports 37*, 3, 971–980.

Lara, J. (2015). *Autism Movement Therapy® Method: Waking up the Brain!* London: Jessica Kingsley Publishers.

LaSalle Network (2015) *LaSalle Network Explores Top Job Interview Trends.* Retrieved on March 8, 2017 from https://thelasallenetwork.com/newsroom/new-lasalle-network-explores-top-job-interview-trends/

Liptak, J. and Allen, P. (2009). *Work Smarts: Using Multiple Intelligences to Make Better Career Choices.* St. Paul, Minnesota: Jist Publishing

Little, A.C., Burriss, R.P., Jones, B.C., and Roberts, S.C. (2007). "Facial appearance affects voting decisions." *Evolution and Human Behavior, 28*, 18–27.

Locsin, A. (n.d.). *Hierarchical Positions in a Typical Corporation.* Retrieved from Chron.com on March 8, 2017 from http://smallbusiness.chron.com/hierarchical-positions-typical-corporation-34491.html

McKnight, P.E. and Kashdan, T.B. (2009). "Purpose in life as a system that creates and sustains health and well-being: An integrative, testable theory." *Review of General Psychology, 13*, 3, 242–251.

MindTools (2011). *Conflict resolution: Using the interest-based relational approach.* Retrieved on March 8, 2017 from www.mindtools.com/pages/article/newLDR_81.htm

Monster (2017). *What's the Difference Between Exempt and Non Exempt Employees.* Retrieved on March 8, 2017 from www.monster.com/career-advice/article/whats-the-difference-between-exempt

Montepare, J.M., and Zebrowitz, L.A. (1998). "Person perception comes of age: The salience and significance of age in social judgments." *Advances in Experimental Social Psychology, 30*, 93–161.

Moore Norman Technology Center Employment Guide. (n.d.). Retrieved December 30, 2016 from https://career-connection.mntc.edu/sites/default/files/public/mntcemploymentguidefy142.pdf

Moraine, P. (2015). *Autism and Everyday Executive Function: A Strengths-Based Approach for Improving Attention, Memory, Organization, and Flexibility.* London: Jessica Kingsley Publishers.

Nolo (2017). *Workers' Compensation Benefits FAQ.* Retrieved on March 8, 2017 from www.nolo.com/legal-encyclopedia/your-right-to-workers-comp-benefits-faq-29093.html

Reference.com (2017). *What is the Purpose of a Human Resources Department?* Retrieved on March 8, 2017 from www.reference.com/business-finance/purpose-human-resources-department-82c1 cc6e20b894b?qo=contentSimilarQuestions

Rosenthal, M., Wallace, G.L., Lawson, R., Wills, M.C., *et al.* (2013). "Impairments in real-world executive function increase from childhood to adolescence in autism spectrum disorders." *Neuropsychology, 27,* 1, 13.

Steger. M.F. (2009) *Meaningful work: What makes work meaningful?* (Psychology Today blog) June 9. Retrieved on March 13, 2017 from www.psychologytoday.com/blog/the-meaning-in-life/200906/meaningful-work

Stoeffel, K., Glamour.com. (2015, April). *How to Date (Responsibly) at Work.* Retrieved online January 16, 2017 from http://www.glamour.com/story/dating-at-work-rules-for-dating-coworkers-tips-advice

UC (University of California) *Berkeley, Career Center. Informational Interviewing (2016).* Retrieved on March 13, 2017 from https://career.berkeley.edu/Info/InfoInterview#benefits

UCLA Mindfulness Research Center (n.d.). Retrieved on March 13, 2017 from http://marc.ucla.edu/about-marc

UCLA Mindfulness Research Center (n.d.). Retrieved on March 13, 2017 from http://marc.ucla.edu/mindful-meditations

United States Department of Labor (n.d.). *Elaws – Employment Law Guide: Laws, Regulations, and Technical Assistance Services.* Retrieved on March 13, 2017 from http://webapps.dol.gov/elaws/elg/

United States Department of Labor (n.d.). *Laws and Regulations.* Retrieved on March 13, 2017 from www.dol.gov/general/topic/disability/laws

United States Department of Labor (n.d.). *Unemployment Insurance.* Retrieved on March 13, 2017 from www.dol.gov/general/topic/unemployment-insurance

United States Department of Labor, Bureau of Labor Statistics (2015). *Occupational Outlook Handbook.* Retrieved on March 10, 2017 from www.bls.gov/ooh/occupation-finder.htm

United States Department of Labor, Bureau of Labor Statistics (2016a). *Table A-6. Employment status of the civilian population by sex, age, and disability status, not seasonally adjusted.* Retrieved on March 13, 2017 from www.bls.gov/news.release/empsit.t06.htm

United States Department of Labor, Bureau of Labor Statistics (2016b). *The American Time Use Survey.* Retrieved on March 10, 2017 from www.bls.gov/tus/charts/leisure.htm

United States Department of Labor, Bureau of Labor Statistics. (May, 2017). *Table A-6. Employment status of the civilian population by sex, age, and disability status, not seasonally adjusted.* Retrieved January 15, 2017 from www.bls.gov/news.release/empsit.t06.htm

United States Department of Labor, Employment & Training Administration (2015a). *Contacts for State UI Tax Information and Assistance.* Retrieved on March 13, 2017 from https://workforcesecurity.doleta.gov/unemploy/agencies.asp

United States Department of Labor, Employment & Training Administration (2015b). *State Unemployment Benefits.* Retrieved on March 10, 2017 from https://workforcesecurity.doleta.gov/unemploy/uifactsheet.asp

United States Department of Labor, Employment and Training Administration, Fact Sheet. (1989, February). *The Worker Adjustment and Retraining Notification Act.* Retrieved March 13, 2107 from www.doleta.gov/programs/factsht/warn.html

United States Department of Labor, Occupational Safety and Health Administration (n.d.). *How to File a Safety Complaint.* Retrieved on March 13, 2017 from www.osha.gov/workers/file_complaint.html

United States Department of Labor, Occupational Safety and Health Administration (2004, Jan). Retrieved on March 13, 2017. www.osha.gov/pls/oshaweb/owadisp.show_document?p_table=OSHACT&p_id=2743

United States Department of Labor, Office of Disability Employment Policy (2013). *Job Accommodation Network. Employees with Autism Spectrum Disorder.* Retrieved on March 13, 2017 from https://askjan.org/media/downloads/ASDA&CSeries.pdf

United States Department of Labor, Office of Workers' Compensation Programs (n.d.). *Division of Federal Employees' Compensation (DFEC).* Retrieved on March 10, 2017 from www.dol.gov/owcp/dfec/regs/compliance/wc.htm

United States Department of Labor, Wage and Hour Division (2015a) *Need Time? The Employee's Guide to the Family and Medical Leave Act.* Retrieved on March 13, 2017 from www.dol.gov/whd/fmla/employeeguide.pdf

United States Department of Labor, Wage and Hour Division (n.d.). *State Labor Laws.* Retrieved on March 10, 2017 from www.dol.gov/whd/state/state.htm

United States Department of Labor, Wage and Hour Division (2017). *Minimum Wage Laws in States.* Retrieved on March 10, 2017 from www.dol.gov/whd/minwage/america.htm

United States Department of Labor, Minimum Wage. (n.d.). Retrieved on March 10, 2017 from https://www.dol.gov/general/topic/wages/minimumwage

United States Department of Labor, Wage and Hour Division. *Compliance Assistance—Wages and the Fair Labor Standards Act (FLSA).* Retrieved online January 15, 2017 from https://www.dol.gov/whd/flsa/efs

U.S. Equal Employment Opportunity Commission (n.d.a). *Facts about the Americans with Disabilities Act.* Retrieved on March 13, 2017 from www.eeoc.gov/eeoc/publications/fs-ada.cfm

U.S. Equal Employment Opportunity Commission (n.d.b). *Harassment.* Retrieved on March 13, 2017 from www.eeoc.gov/laws/types/harassment.cfm

U.S. Equal Employment Opportunity Commission (n.d.c). *Sexual Harassment.* Retrieved on March 13, 2017 from https://www.eeoc.gov/laws/types/sexual_harassment.cfm

U.S. Equal Employment Opportunity Commission. (2002, May). *United States Department of Justice, Civil Rights Division. Americans with Disabilities Act, Questions and Answers.* Retrieved March 13, 2017 from www.ada.gov/archive/q&aeng02.htm

U.S. Equal Employment Opportunity Commission. (2017, February). *United States Department of Justice, Civil Rights Division. Americans with Disabilities Act, Questions and Answers.* Retrieved March 13, 2017 from www.ada.gov/archive/q&aeng02.htm

U.S Equal Employment Opportunity Commission. (2002, October). *Enforcement Guidance: Reasonable Accommodation and Undue Hardship Under the Americans with Disabilities Act.* Retrieved March 13, 2017 from https://www.eeoc.gov/policy/docs/accommodation.html

United States Internal Revenue Service (2016a). *Employer and Employee Responsibilities—Employment Tax Enforcement.* Retrieved on March 13, 2017 from www.irs.gov/uac/employer-and-employee-responsibilities-employment-tax-enforcement

United States Internal Revenue Service (2016b). *Independent Contractor Defined.* Retrieved on March 13, 2017 from www.irs.gov/businesses/small-businesses-self-employed/independent-contractor-defined

University of California Berkeley, Career Center (2016) *Informational Interviewing.* Retrieved on March 13, 2017 from https://career.berkeley.edu/Info/InfoInterview#benefits

Willis, J. and Todorov, A. (2006). "First Impressions: Making up Your Mind after a 100-Ms Exposure to a Face." *Psychological Science, 17,* 7, 592–598.

Wright, S. (2009). *Three components of meaningful work.* Retrieved on March 13, 2017, from www.meaningandhappiness.com/meaningful-work/360/

Yager, J. (1999),.*Friendships: The Power of Friendship and How it Shapes our Lives.* Stamford, CT: Hannacroix Creek Books.

Zebrowitz, L.A., and McDonald, S.M. (1991). "The impact of litigants' baby-facedness and attractiveness on adjudications in small claims courts." *Law and Behavior, 15,* 6, 603–623.

Index

on-the-job support 103
parties 82–3
planned social activities 82
remembering information about
    others 81–2
sharing information about self 81
socializing outside workplace 84
SODA strategy 86–7
social events, dressing for 61–2
social media presence
    Facebook 76
    overview of 70–1, 74–6
    personal websites 76
    Pinterest 62, 76–7
    Twitter 76
    see also business websites
social security number 49–50
social security tax 95
SODA strategy 86–7
soft skills 36
spatial intelligence 46
"splintered skill" sets 17, 42
spreadsheets 57
state income tax 95
state unemployment insurance benefits
    96–7
statistics, unemployment 18, 22
stress management 84–8, 103
structure, from work 29–30
supervisor supports 102

Tasks, Google 56–7
taxes 95–6

temp jobs 72–3
thank you notes 67
theory of mind 33–4, 86–7
Thomas-Kilmann Conflict Mode
    Instrument 107–8
time management 64–5, 102
Twitter 76

understanding/awareness of autism 37
unemployment insurance benefits 96–7
unemployment statistics 18, 22
United States Department of Labor 22

vocational education 19–20, 21–2
volunteering 72

W-4 form 50
whistleblower protection 98
wifi 125
word-processing 57
Work Smarts Assessment 45–8
Worker Adjustment and Retraining
    Notification Act (WARN) 99
worker's compensation 97
Workplace Readiness Workshop
    candidates in 38
    classroom meetings 38–9, 127–33
    field trips 39, 134–42

YouTube 57–8

Luke Rose